BOSUN'S BAG

ADLARD COLES
Bloomsbury Publishing Plc
50 Bedford Square, London, WC1B 3DP, UK
29 Earlsfort Terrace, Dublin 2, Ireland

BLOOMSBURY, ADLARD COLES and the Adlard Coles logo are trademarks of Bloomsbury Publishing Plc

First published in Great Britain 2024

Copyright © Tom Cunliffe, 2024
Illustrations © Martyn Mackrill, 2024

Tom Cunliffe and Martyn Mackrill have asserted their right under the Copyright, Designs and Patents Act, 1988, to be identified as Authors of this work.

Some of the content in this book originally appeared in *Classic Boat* magazine

All rights reserved. No part of this publication may be reproduced or transmitted in any form or by any means, electronic or mechanical, including photocopying, recording, or any information storage or retrieval system, without prior permission in writing from the publishers

Bloomsbury Publishing Plc does not have any control over, or responsibility for, any third-party websites referred to or in this book. All internet addresses given in this book were correct at the time of going to press. The author and publisher regret any inconvenience caused if addresses have changed or sites have ceased to exist, but can accept no responsibility for any such changes

A catalogue record for this book is available from the British Library
Library of Congress Cataloguing-in-Publication data has been applied for

ISBN: HB: 978-1-3994-1189-9; ePub: 978-1-3994-1190-5; ePDF: 978-1-3994-1192-9

10 9 8 7 6 5 4 3 2 1

Typeset in Garamond Premier by Lee-May Lim
Printed and bound in India by Replika Press Pvt. Ltd.

To find out more about our authors and books
visit www.bloomsbury.com and sign up for our newsletters

BY TOM CUNLIFFE
AND MARTYN MACKRILL

BOSUN'S BAG

A TREASURY OF PRACTICAL WISDOM FOR THE TRADITIONAL BOATER

ADLARD COLES

LONDON · OXFORD · NEW YORK · NEW DELHI · SYDNEY

CONTENTS

Introduction 6

1 | Sails 12

Setting a single-luff spinnaker 14
Tricing up or scandalising a
    gaff mainsail 17
Yankee jibs 19
Thoughts on topsails 21
The mysterious watersail 24
Setting up the foretriangle when
    sailing to windward 26
Dragging the clew 29
Boomed staysail – friend or foe? 31

2 | Rigging 34

Ratlines 34
The problem of the crane 38
Making sheer poles work 40
The humble burton 42
Spreaders 45
Baggywrinkle 47
Mast rake and boom angle 50
Setting up deadeyes: the excellent
    and the ludicrous 52
Housing bowsprits 53
Dyarchy forestay 56
Mainsheet arrangements 58
Topping lift 61
Artificial hemp 62

3 | Working the ship 64
The old-fashioned lizard............................ 66
Mast hoops.. 68
Reefing the main....................................... 69
Harbour-stowing the staysail.................... 72
Tiller lines... 74
Stanchions and guardrails......................... 76
Stowing sails... 79
Sail ties... 81
Flaking for the drop.................................. 82
Stopping the rattle.................................... 83

4 | Navigation 84
Box the compass...................................... 84
A classic logbook..................................... 86
Tap the glass.. 88
Thinking outside the box.......................... 89
Back to basics.. 89

5 | Miscellaneous 90
Fiddles.. 92
Oil lamps.. 94
Christmas Eve without electricity.............. 99
Chain plates – internal and external 102
Weather helm and movable ballast......... 103
Boom gallows.. 105
Windvane... 106
Keep awake 109
Using up old sawdust 110
Mastheads akimbo................................. 110

6 | Maintenance 112
Slushing down and other unctions 114
Deck leaks.. 116
Traditional deck seams........................... 119
Pouring pitch.. 120
Stopping up.. 121
Maintaining brightwork........................... 122
Wooden blocks – maintaining
   performance 126
Boot tops and wale strakes 131
Boats in winter 132
Proper job – dealing with the unlikely..... 136
Useful materials..................................... 138

7 | Seamanship 140
Towing dinghies in a following sea 142
The honest fisherman 143
How to sail an anchor out....................... 146
Drying out.. 149
Flag etiquette... 151
Burgees.. 152
Give us a swig, Mate.............................. 154
Sculling.. 157
Hoisting the dinghy aboard 158
Purchases – an extra part for nothing 161
Bull ropes... 162
Securing a rope...................................... 163
Marking the anchor cable....................... 166
A bullseye aloft...................................... 167
Offset propellers.................................... 167

Glossary 168
Index 173

INTRODUCTION

I was born in the immediate aftermath of World War II. In those days, boats were mainly of timber construction. Plywood had appeared and steel was around in small numbers, but most were still built plank-on-frame. Cotton and flax sails were everywhere, auxiliary engines in sailing craft were notoriously unreliable, and although rudimentary radio direction finding had spilled over from the hostilities, little had changed in navigation during the two centuries since Harrison's chronometer delivered longitude to the ordinary sailor.

Development on the water had followed a slow, natural progression from the man paddling across a river on a log to the complex hull forms and sky-scraping rigs of the golden era of yachting. Using only natural materials that came readily to hand or could be forged from basic metals, boats and wooden ships had achieved a remarkable degree of sophistication. Until so-called Corinthian yachting began to take hold around 1900, the art and science of maintaining such craft at sea fell, in the Navy, to the 'lower deck'. Outside the military, it was the paid yacht hands or the fishermen and pilot boat crews of small working craft. A vessel of any size had its official or unofficial bosun, whose task it was to keep things running smoothly.

Such men were guardians of the wisdom of ages; their tools were simple and their skills were not book-learned, they stemmed from a life at sea that began as a child, watching and learning all the way. Nothing was beyond their ingenuity, and resourcefulness was

RIGHT: The 1911 Bristol Channel pilot cutter *Hirta* in mid-Atlantic, in 1984. The figures in the cockpit are the author and his family. The painting now hangs in his daughter's house

their watchword. They knew how much red lead powder to mix with linseed oil putty to make up a seam stopping that would survive summer sun and arctic chill. They could caulk a leaking deck and they understood whether to use tarred oakum or soft white cotton. Working a long splice into a chafed main brace so that the rope would pass through a block and never let go was nothing they couldn't handle, while stripping that same block and servicing it could be done in their sleep.

They'd steer a ship or a boat close-hauled through a difficult sea with artistry, then instruct a young foredeck hand in the mysterious relationship between jib and staysail on a cutter. Meanwhile, their American brothers were setting a fisherman staysail between the topmasts of a schooner, deciding on instinct whether to send it up to weather or to leeward of the fore gaff.

A good bosun could survey a deck in chaos following some major mishap and always find that vital sense of priorities for putting things to rights. Shakespeare understood this well. In the opening storm-at-sea scene in *The Tempest*, things are looking bad for the ship; the crew are working flat out to keep her afloat when one of the passengers grabs the bosun and demands that he save the nobles aboard. The gentleman is rewarded with a short-shrift response that would have sat comfortably with my old-fashioned mentors:

'REMEMBER WHOM THOU HAST ABOARD,' SAYS THE REPRESENTATIVE OF THE 'QUALITY'.

'NONE THAT I LOVE MORE THAN MYSELF,' REPLIES THE BOSUN. 'YOU ARE A COUNSELLOR; IF YOU CAN COMMAND THESE ELEMENTS TO SILENCE, AND WORK THE PEACE OF THE PRESENT, WE WILL NOT HAND A ROPE MORE; USE YOUR AUTHORITY: IF YOU CANNOT, GIVE THANKS YOU HAVE LIVED SO LONG, AND MAKE YOURSELF READY IN YOUR CABIN FOR THE MISCHANCE OF THE HOUR...'

Turning his back on the gent, the bosun promptly organises the hands to lower the topmasts, a remarkable feat performed regularly at sea in heavy weather as recently as the 19th century.

Quite what Shakespeare's bosun might have made of the denizens of a 21st-century yacht marina is anybody's guess, but there's no doubt that a major revolution has taken place in my lifetime. Fibreglass and stainless steel rigging arose in the postwar years and soon swept the board. With it came production runs of vessels that worked well enough but lacked the character of their

LEFT: Pilot cutters making an early start. The crew of an original are about to lower the oil-fired riding light and weigh anchor. In the foreground, the easel has been set up on the deck of a replica with the staysail bent on ready to go

forebears. Owners bought and sold them as they might a family car and while they still have to be maintained, this now demands a different set of skills. The level of expertise with natural things that were once one of the glories of boat ownership have been set aside, together with the traditional boats that are now a rarity. The skills and sheer hard labour involved in looking after them in harbour and at sea have been confined to a select band, but the worm is turning. In addition to rescuing ancient classics from remote mud berths or keeping yachts going that have somehow survived the decades, a new generation is quietly demanding a range of traditional-style craft that suit the changing times.

Not everyone, it seems, is content to sail a yacht designed by a committee and sold in a boat show without ever being seen in the water. Bermudan rig, so efficient on the right sort of hull, is being bypassed by some as the knee-jerk option, replacing it with a gaff-rig alternative on a hull that wouldn't have looked sorely out of place 100 years ago. Fibreglass gaffers and Bermudan classics offer busy modern owners the choice of having a boat that looks right, but relieves them of the annual workup that is fitting out a tidy wooden yacht. The new yachts still have a certain amount of 'bosunry' in them and they liven up the coastal scene by giving their owners a boat that actually has to be sailed, not merely presented to the wind.

Meanwhile, back in the real world of wooden planking, I've often pondered on the sheer scale of the labour involved in rubbing down topsides, followed by caulking, seam-stopping and filling any knocks the boat received last summer. Then it's time to brush on an undercoat and see how well you've done. That will show up any imperfections. It's a test of character now to get out the stopping once more, rub down and try again. Finally, after yet another rub-down, one or two coats of yacht enamel can be applied. If luck's on your side, it'll be dry before it rains.

When considering the joys of turning in a tapered eye splice in a new three-strand rope, or deciding where to position a staysail sheet fairlead, it doesn't do to forget the hours with aching arms that are an integral part of the traditional bosun's bag of skills. But there's satisfaction in the graft. Rather than looking at the totality of the task facing you, it helps to break it down into achievable sections and take them one at a time. One face of a hatch to be varnished might be manageable, or perhaps a length of topsides that can be stopped up before moving the trestles along to the next. One by one, they are dealt with until they're all done. Then you can sit back and contemplate the truth that confounds the smart sailors from the production boaters who walk past your efforts and can only say, 'Looks like a lot of work.' It's tempting to reply, 'More work than you'll ever be good for, Sunshine,' but it's better just to nod, because you know something they never will. When it comes to boating, the more you put in, the more you get out.

This book started its life many years ago with a phone call between me and Rob Peake who was then editor of *Classic Boat* magazine. He had concluded that while the industry professionals were as skilled as they were back in 1850, there was something of a black hole in hands-on knowledge among some owners and would-be owners of traditional boats. Since I'd spent the best part of 50 years keeping such vessels on the high seas, Rob imagined I'd know a thing or two and could put together a useful column on the matter. I set him straight over my own levels of expertise, admitting that I had served no apprenticeship other than the one delivered by the sea.

Fortunately, having been at it longer than most, I'd had plenty of opportunity to learn from the men and women who went before us. Some were professionals like a notable yard foreman, one was a Royal Navy Petty Officer, another was an elderly Yankee schooner captain who had served on the Grand Banks. Then there was the company of old-fashioned yachtsmen still around the yards in the early 1970s who had picked up their own expertise from their fathers and grandfathers. All of these dealt me in to a steady stream of knowledge going back to the beginnings of seafaring. Writing this book to pass on something of what I've learned has been a privilege.

The second real joy of it has been collaborating with my friend Martyn Mackrill, another sailor who has truly 'done his time'. There are many who paint pictures of boats, ships and the sea, but few who understand it as he does. The way he produces an image of a sailor heaving on a rope is uncanny; it succeeds because he has been there himself. As we've been putting this book together, he and his wife Bryony are in the final stages of personally restoring a substantial Fife-built yacht. There's nobody quite like Martyn. We're lucky to have him.

So dip into the bag now. Whatever you're sailing, I hope you'll find something to enrich your passion, and even if my words fall short, Martyn's paintings will surely never fail to delight.

By way of a valediction, may your ship be well looked after from top to bottom. May her burgee halyard never chafe through and may her garboards stay tight beneath the mast step.

CHAPTER ONE
SAILS

It's always interesting to study how Bermudan rig steadily diverged from its parent, gaff, when it first arose early in the 20th century. Initially, foretriangles remained more or less as they were, but as years passed, they slimmed down from three or more headsails on large racing yachts to the efficient single jib of the sloop. Mainsails increased their aspect ratio, growing taller, slimmer and ever more powerful until, shortly before World War II, someone – legend has it Uffa Fox – devised the kicking strap, later termed the vang, to hold the boom under control as it tried to sky and spoil sail shape off the wind. Thereafter, apart from ever-improving materials and gear, things have not altered a lot. It is mainly in gaff rig that the fascination of traditional sailing lives on.

In its most refined forms gaff rig is almost infinitely flexible. Tricing up main tacks, lowering peaks, dropping staysails to continue under main and jib alone, reefing and so on make for highly satisfying manoeuvring, while hoisting a topsail can turbocharge a boat that is looking for sail area where it really counts. For reasons of space and for a certain lack of personal expertise, I have not covered the wonderful world of the lugger here, nor have I discussed the phenomenally versatile sprit rig favoured by the Thames sailing barge. This is a pity, but one cannot do everything in this life.

RIGHT: Setting a classic single-luff spinnaker. The sail has been hoisted clear of everything and the two men by the mast have just hauled out the tack to the pole end to break out any stops

Setting a single-luff spinnaker

Sailors of today having their first taste of big classic racing may be surprised when the downwind canvas appears. They'll have been studying Beken photographs of the great yachts before World War I with those enormous single-luff spinnakers, so it will come as a shock when the modern asymmetric goes whistling out to the bowsprit end and hoists to leeward with enough slack in the tack line for it to drift beyond the shadow of the mainsail. On anything except a dead-square run, these sails are a major improvement on their historic predecessors. Handling them is comparatively simple too, although on a J-class yacht or a 160-foot schooner, 'simple' is a relative term. Such mighty sails are not for the fainthearted.

Notwithstanding this general progress, classic single-luff spinnakers set emphatically on the windward side of the boat are still seen, either to keep tradition, or because race regulations prohibit 21st-century answers to the age-old issue of running in a fore-and-aft rigged vessel. And a grand sight they are.

Their booms are so long that they are usually kept with the heel permanently attached forward of the gooseneck and the pole hoisted out of the way. Often the outboard end stows near, at, or even above the hounds, making it possible for the masthead man to secure it when it's off watch.

The gear on the pole is similar to that on a modern spinnaker boom, in that it has a topping lift, an after guy and a foreguy. However, there is a major difference. Today's poles are set well clear of the water, giving the foreguy a strong downward component to its pull angle. This is critical to the setting of the sail, allowing it to be carried with the pole virtually at the forestay on a shy reach. The traditional pole is much lower. It is also a lot longer, and so the angle it makes with the foreguy does little if anything to hold the pole down against the pull of the sail. Set as it ideally should be, more or less dead downwind, this doesn't create much in the way of problems, but if the helmsman loses concentration and lets the yacht start to round up, watch out!

HOISTING THE SAIL

Procedures vary for hoisting the sail, but in general it will go something like this:

- Potential drama can be side-stepped by stopping up the sail with 'rotten' caulking cotton or rubber bands before letting it get near the halyard. Start at the head, then work luff and leech through your hands, stopping the sail as you go, until you reach the foot. Leave the tack and clew clear of the bottom stop. A really big sail may need two or even four people on this job, but a more modest example can be pre-snuffed by one honest soul tucked away out of the rain in the saloon.

- Release the pole from aloft and lower away on the topping lift. Ease the guy and haul away on the foreguy so that it is about 45 degrees forward of athwartships while still well topped-up.

- Shackle on the halyard, passing the line on the correct, windward, side of the forestay. There must be a swivel on the head of the sail.

- Bend the outhaul onto the tack. Note that the tack is sent out to the pole end, making it, by definition, the lower windward corner of the sail. The outhaul will pass through a single turning block shackled or stropped to the outboard end of the pole. Sometimes the outhaul is rigged via a leathered and well-tallowed traveller similar to that used for a bowsprit jib, but more often it is set 'flying'.

- Secure the sheet 'pro tem' to some strong point on the lee side just abaft the mast, or bring it through a fairlead in a similar position. On some boats, the sheet is led very close to the mast, and on small yachts it can even end up to weather of the spar. Wherever it lands, however, the sheet must remain on the same side of the forestay as the rest of the gear. In this, it differs radically from the modern 'balloon' spinnaker.

- Make sure the topmast runner is set up, then hoist the sail as smartly as possible to the topmast head. When the halyard is 'up and stretched', haul out the tack. It's more than likely the stops will start to let go before the tack reaches the block, but as long as it's almost home, this won't matter a lot. If the sail does fill prematurely because the sheet is tight, let it off so the luff lifts and give the outhaul all you've got.

- With the tack 'home' in its block, haul the guy aft and square the pole, now parallel with the water, easing the foreguy gingerly as you go. Let the sheet well off as you do this if there's a stiffish breeze, to stop the pole from kicking up.

- When the sail is up with the tack home and the pole squared, trim the sheet in the same way as you would for any other sail and 'Oh Lord, let her go!'

TRICING UP OR SCANDALISING A GAFF MAINSAIL

One of the hidden benefits of gaff rig is that shortening sail drastically in a couple of seconds comes in two exciting flavours, neither of which is available to the Bermudan hordes. Tricing up is, in my opinion, the superior of the two, but in order to execute it the sail must be loose-footed on its boom and must be held into the mast by hoops. Given these two premises, all that's required is a tricing line run from the tack of the sail up to the gaff jaws, around a turning block secured up there, and back down to the deck.

To ditch a third of the sail's area in no time at all, simply cast off the tack and heave up the tricing line. Because the peak halyards remain undisturbed, the leech tension doesn't change so there's no need to set up the topping lift. The aft section of the sail and the lovely flat run-off to the leech still pull with uncompromised aerodynamics and the boat simply sails more upright and a bit slower. There's also an unexpected spin-off that comes for free. The helmsman's view is improved by 100% once the tack is up and out of the way. There's more about tricing on page 68.

Many of the gaffers I sail on these days do not have mast hoops, so this glorious option disappears. The alternative of using a well-tallowed lacing works well enough to stop the sail from escaping when hoisting or lowering, but that's about all it does. It is a poor substitute in every respect, but it's cheap, convenient to rig and many owners who might wish in light of experience to change are stuck with it until the next time the mast is out. That's the moment to get shot of the lacing for good and equip with a nice set of hoops.

Fortunately, however, all is not lost. Even a laced-on main can be depowered in a hurry by dropping the peak in a process often called 'scandalising'.

Scandalising is a lot less elegant than tricing up and, for a similar reduction in sail area, the difference in performance between it and tricing is dramatic. The head of a gaff sail goes some way to increasing the luff length, so the sail loses power as well as area once robbed of the straight edge of the gaff. Because part of the sail may now be flogging, it's not a state of affairs one would want to hold all night long in a hard breeze. Nonetheless, scandalising can still be useful.

LEFT: The gaff mainsail is supremely adaptable to changing conditions. While a neatly tied reef is always the long-term answer to a rising breeze, scandalising the sail by topping the boom and easing away the peak halyard offers an instant and substantial reduction under reasonable control

A well-rigged gaffer with hoops, a loose foot and twin topping lifts can make her mainsail virtually disappear by tricing up, then scandalising. This isn't something you'd do every day, but the technique is priceless when picking up moorings or anchoring with wind against tide. The modern yacht can drop her main and cruise in under a half-rolled genoa. Most will even tack without a main. Not so the gaffer. She needs her main up almost to the end to keep way on, but she still must be rid of it as she heads into the tide for the final pickup, because at this point it won't spill wind and she can't stop while it's setting.

Scandalising alone is often not enough for this refinement, but there's nothing quite like it when caught out by a squall. And when the wind has settled back to where it should be, you've only to sway the peak back up, fine-tune the leech with the halyard purchase and let off the topping lift, while your three-cornered chums are shaking out reefs and struggling to discover why the pennants have somehow got themselves stuck.

SCANDALISING

Here's the procedure:

- Set up the weather topping lift. Since the peak halyard is effectively supporting the boom via the leech of the sail, the spar is going to drop like a brick when the halyards are eased away. If you've only a single topping lift you'd better hope it's on the windward side of the sail and consider rigging a pair at the next refit.

- Ease the throat halyard a little way. When you let go the peak, the geometry of the sail goes to pieces, a hard 'girt' often appears between clew and throat and a strain comes on the luff of the sail. This can manifest itself in terms of an unfair stretching, or even damage in way of the throat cringle. Easing the halyard to settle the throat a few inches before ditching the peak protects against this.

- Finally, let off the peak halyard. How low you let the gaff go is a matter of taste. All the way does no harm, except that the lower it goes, the worse the angle for the halyards when it's time to heave it back up again.

Yankee jibs

Gaff-rig offers a feast of opportunities for creative sailors to cram on canvas, but, of all the options, two are akin to kicking in wind-powered turbochargers. If a schoonerman challenges me with 'what about the gollywobbler?' I'll hold up my hands, but so long as we leave that monster of legend and mystery out, you can't beat the jackyarder and the full-hoist jib topsail, or Yankee. Omitting jackyarders on this occasion, I'm concentrating on the mighty Yankee and we'd better start by defining the beast. It tacks down to the bowsprit end, or close above it. The head goes to the topmast head. Don't ask about the sheet for now. Its lead is often a movable feast, so we'll discuss it later.

All sorts of boats set sails called 'Yankees'. My modern classic Bermudan cutter has a Yankee on the outer forestay roller and many a gaffer of my acquaintance has dragged one out of the forepeak when speed drops and closing time beckons. I used to wonder about the name, until I started researching American pilot schooners.

BELOW: Two yachts from the Golden Age in light airs, both setting full-hoist power-house 'Yankee' jib topsails

The *America* was a direct sister of the 1850s New York schooners which certainly knew how to set clouds of canvas, but it was only as the century drew onwards that the two-topmast rig came into vogue and, with it, the full-hoist jib topsail. I don't doubt that these sails were used elsewhere, but it was in North America that they blossomed into their full glory. The ones on display in photos of the powerful *Hesper* and her sisters are immense and they all had them. As did the Gloucester fishing schooners, and Herreshoff's *Westward* when she stomped across to beat up Kaiser Bill in Kiel. This must be where the name originates.

Now that's sorted out, let's look into how these sails can best be handled.

Every-day jibs for working gaffers on the east side of the Atlantic are set 'flying'. They are only attached at tack, head and clew, relying entirely on halyard tension to provide the tight luff that all headsails must have. So long as they are set from a relatively solid bowsprit and a well-stayed lower mast, the arrangement works reasonably well.

When it comes to jib topsails, be they Yankees or more modest upper-air kites, setting one flying is a non-starter. There is just too much space between bowsprit end and masthead to be able to crank up the luff sufficiently. Even if some muscleman managed it, the resulting compression loads on relatively light spars would be ruinous. All 'jib tops' are therefore hanked to an outer, or topmast, forestay. This means that some poor masher has to go out to the bowsprit end. On a sail-training cutter like the 55-ton *Jolie Brise* this is not too bad, because such craft usually feature bowsprit netting. This not only creates more than the mere illusion of security, it also constrains the body of the sail while it is being bent on or off.

If you don't have netting, you need a bigger crew to feed the sail out, possibly stopped up with rotten cotton, with two or three hands stationed along the spar. Serious classics generally don't find this a problem because, not only do they ship big crews on race days, they also carry a ready supply of fit young professionals for whom regular trips down a bowsprit into the 'green room' are a rite of passage I remember only too well.

All fine and dandy, but what if you don't have a big crew, bowsprit netting, or a ready supply of waterproof youngsters itching to go? Here's what we did on *Westernman*, my Irens-designed 41-footer, well-known in the Channel for her ability to carry sail. I picked the idea up from my friend Simon when he owned *Chloe May*. Both boats crossed the North Atlantic and were not simply darlings of the summer day.

The topmast forestay ended in a hard eye a foot or two above the bowsprit end. To this was shackled a length of flexible steel wire. Today, a better solution would be Spectra core with Brummel splices. This was rove through a turning block on the cranse iron, brought inboard over the stemhead breast hooks and secured to the bitts with a 4:1 tackle. When jib-top or Yankee time came, we let go the tackle, unhooked it and hitched a lightweight messenger to the flex wire, saving the overhauling of miles of purchase. The topmast forestay was grabbed with a long boathook if it didn't fall to hand, and we were ready to go, safe inside the bulwarks. If there was doubt about the security of the topmast with no forestay –

usually there wasn't – we'd turn briefly off the wind. The tack or tack-line was shackled to the eye in the stay, the sail was hanked on, sheets, halyard and downhaul attached. Plenty of slack was now overhauled, the stay was pulled back into place and set up hard. All that remained was to hoist away and sheet in. Dropping the sail with that vital downhaul was the reverse.

What about the sheets then? It's possible, of course, to run these directly to a conveniently placed cavil or cleat, but a 'live' sheet on a Yankee can be a one-way ticket to hospital. It's always going to be a hard pull, but if the sheet is run through a turning block as far aft as possible, it's no longer lethal. This may site the lead so far aft that the leech opens too much. The tidiest answer is then to pass the sheet through a lizard – a bullseye on the end of a lanyard – so that the bight can be hove down to get the ideal sheeting angle for maximum power. If this is a step too far in complication, just lob the tail of a topping lift or halyard purchase over the bight of the sheet and pull down. The effect is the same but it's 'nil points' for elegance. See page 66 for further details.

Thoughts on topsails

Back in the days when the mainstream yachting magazines still wrote about gaff rig, *Yachting Monthly*'s editor, the late lamented J D Sleightholme, had something to say about topsails. I can't remember his exact words, but the gist was this: 'Topsails. We hoist them, tweak them, glower at them, stamp on them and toss them into the nearest skip. Then we go out and order a bigger one...' The story of my life. Yours too, I'll bet, if you sail a gaffer.

Comparing a gaff topsail with a Bermudan mainsail is a bit like the contrast between a chart plotter and a radar screen. The plotter is child's play, while radar demands considerable user skills. Hoist a typical three-cornered mainsail, give it some vang, sheet in and off you jolly well go. Not so a gaff topsail. Getting one up can be easy, but for some it's an on-going nightmare. Once aloft, persuading it to pull sweetly is as much an art as a science.

A year or two back I was chatting with our artist, Martyn Mackrill, whose watercolour of a jackyard topsail graces the next page. Martyn was considering a topsail for the 31-foot Maurice Griffiths cutter *Nightfall* he then owned and was wondering about the details. His dilemma flushed out some random observations. With no topmast and a typically short masthead, he needed a yard to carry the luff above the halyard sheave to make for a well-proportioned sail. So, how long should the yard be, and ought there also to be a club yard at the clew to extend the sail beyond the gaff, making it a jackyarder?

LUFF YARD OR FULL JACKYARDER?

That extra yard looks sexy and, in my experience, it powers up the sail more than the additional area would suggest. However, once a topsail has two spars, hoisting and lowering it becomes more of a production. There's more weight, of course, but the propensity of a club yard to foul peak halyards, gaff spans, topping lifts, the fall of the sheet and the owner's wife's parasol is so great that hoisting is best approached as a set piece. So long as the yacht can be held with the wind fine on one bow while hoisting to leeward, the club has a decent chance of slipping up cleanly when nobody is watching. If this can't be achieved – and I appreciate all boats are different – weeping is likely to be the bosun's portion as he looks round for some poor sailor to blame for the lash-up.

A sail with a single luff spar, on the other hand, has every chance of a fair passage aloft, whether to windward, to leeward or head to wind. To windward, snagging is a short-odds possibility but, given practice, a smart crew can often overcome this. To leeward it's easy, except that you can't see what's going on because the bunt of the mainsail blocks the view.

So much for single-yard benefits when hoisting. At dropping time, the over-riding advantage is that, with sensible forethought, a single yard in regular use can be more or less guaranteed to come down smartly in a squall or rising wind, even in the dark. The same definitely can't be said for a jackyarder. The opportunities for the club to grab something it shouldn't are endless and can lead to the ultimate solution of sending a boy of little consequence aloft to walk the gaff and sort it out. For a cruiser, therefore, the jackyarder is best seen as a party-time sail. For the racer, the turbo-charged power is not to be denied and the boys just have to live with the knitting.

HOW LONG IS YOUR YARD?

Having decided against the club, the next issue was, how long was Martyn's luff yard to be? I've found that, if weight is kept to a minimum, a yard that runs most of the length of the luff guarantees a straight leading edge. It should extend the masthead sufficiently to make a healthy upward angle from the gaff end. Like my own 32-foot *Saari* back in the 1970s, *Nightfall* is small enough to choose this option.

Larger craft generally have to use a relatively shorter yard that balances at the sheave but only carries the upper half of the luff. The canvas stretched out below the yard is therefore free to drift away from the mast when the sheet is hauled out to the gaff end. This wrecks the shape of the sail, so the luff is usually controlled with a tight line called a leader running from a peak halyard band to the deck. The lower part of the luff is hanked to this and the yard is attached to the halyard. It's a compromise and it works, but compared with a simple, long yard it's a lot more cumbersome.

LEFT: The masthead man checks the luff on a fully sparred jackyard topsail

OVERLAP

The next query was about overlap. On a 30-footer, the topsail clew is best pitched around six to eight inches away from the gaff end. This allows the sheet to be hardened with a rising breeze, keeping the sail nice and flat. The result is that the outboard end of the foot – the edge running along the gaff – has a gap between it and the spar. The tack of the sail is best cut twelve inches or so below the gaff jaws so the line of the foot crosses the gaff around halfway. Conventionally, the bottom foot or two of the luff continues below the lower end of the topsail yard, creating elbow room at the hounds. This overlap looks good; it allows the sail to be set in varying conditions and supplies a little extra grunt.

THE LEADER

This is a length of line or wire spliced round the upper mast and set up on the deck, close to the spar. Hank on the lower luff of the topsail. The upper part relies on halyard tension. On craft up to 40 tons this can be rigged around a turning block on deck, then tensioned, as per the Dyarchy forestay (page 56).

DOWNHAULING

As for the vital downhaul that keeps the luff yard bolt upright after the halyard is belayed, a 30-footer with a hefty crew might get away with no purchase at all. It's not difficult to rig a whip, however, and a 40-footer will be grateful for 4:1. My 20-ton *Westernman* actually had 8:1. She pointed like a modern yacht and went like smoke fleeing a summer gale.

THE MYSTERIOUS WATERSAIL

All of us carry in our heads and hearts images from our yesterdays. One of mine dates from the Arcadian years when I lived on my ancient cutter on the Hamble River and a pal owned *Piskie*, a tiny Falmouth quay punt. Late one perfect spring afternoon I was beating westwards down the Solent on the sea breeze. A lively force four ruffled the water so it sparkled like diamonds, and running down on me from the Needles came *Piskie*. Backlit, she looked two notches bigger than she actually was. A jackyarder reached for the sky, a monster balloon staysail was poled out to windward, her boom was squared away and under it, pulling like a young horse, was a watersail, its clew kissing the brine as she rolled gently under the press of canvas. I'd never seen a watersail before and, as the little yawl swept by, I resolved that I'd have one rigged before the next gaffers' race. I did, and I kept one ready for action from that day until I sold my last gaffer.

A watersail is triangular. Fortuitously, as it happens, its proportions are similar to a high-clewed jib that's designed to be set flying. It carries its luff along the main boom. The tack is outboard and the head generally inboard of the rail. The clew should stand as close to a calmish sea as may be arranged with a lightweight sheet secured at some suitable place on deck well aft. The net effect of its drive is, it must be said, not great, but it does wonders for crew morale and is without equal for psyching out the opposition. If you're thinking that these sorts of things

are not worth paying for, you would be in a comfortable majority. I have yet to meet anyone who asked a sailmaker to build him a watersail. So here's what you do:

Delve into the sail locker and rouse out a small jib with a luff length more or less the same as your boom. If you don't have one, something will turn up for pennies at the local boat jumble. To rig it, lash a block to the boom end and reeve a length of old rope through it as an outhaul. Bring both ends in to somewhere near the gooseneck. Find something light but reasonably strong to act as a sheet and an odd bit of stuff for the head. Now, run the boat square off downwind. The sail only functions on or near a dead run because there's no appreciable aerofoil. It just shoves the boat along. Attach the sheet, secure the tack to the outhaul, heave it out all the way and make it fast. Pull hard on the head to snug the luff up against the boom. Goodness only knows how you'll secure this corner; maybe to a mast spider-band, perhaps just a turn around the mast itself if the sail's a bit on the big side. It's a lash-up and every boat is different. When the luff is running in a straight line, bring the sheet aft and haul it just hard enough to lift the clew clear of the water, sort out somewhere to tie it off, and away you go.

A watersail is better too long in the luff than too short. On one of my boats, the smallest jib over-ran the gooseneck by three feet with the tack all the way out to the mainsheet iron. My crew just wrapped it around the mast before making it off. It worked perfectly.

One final word of warning. With a respectable running sail poled out to weather and a watersail drawing nicely under the boom, visibility ahead from the helm will be absolute zero. Find someone you can trust to look out, and keep him off the rum until you've blown away the opposition and taken the gun for first home.

Setting up the foretriangle when sailing to windward

Back in the mid-1990s I was in a pub discussing the spec for *Westernman* with Nigel Irens, her designer. *Westernman* is a heavy displacement gaff cutter inspired by pilot boats of the Bristol Channel. No compromise was made in her underwater profile, but, unlike her progenitors, she has outside ballast. This allows her to carry a correspondingly high-aspect ratio rig with gratifying results. As we sketched her out on the back of a menu card, I asked Nigel how high she might point.

The boat was intended for long-distance cruising, and he was quick to remind me of what we both knew too well. Nobody who's been there wants the unpleasantness of sailing a 40-foot boat at six knots 40 degrees off the true wind with a thousand miles to go, so who cares? The breeze is bound to shift in due course anyway. The story is a different one when beating home at the end of a weekend. That's when we need to point up and foot fast, and that's where many a gaffer falls short. They vary widely, of course, but whether they started life as race boats, oyster dredgers or fibreglass yachts built last year, they all share the same issues.

The mainsail and the topsail are

important, obviously, but they can be saved for another day. The real crunch lies in the foretriangle. Schooners, ketches, cutters and sloops; none of them goes upwind without headsails. Only catboats achieve this by a process that remains shrouded in mystery. Setting the genoa on a close-hauled Bermudan production cruiser is largely a matter of grinding it in until the leech is just off the spreaders while making sure the sheeting angle is correct. Nothing to it really. Life on a gaffer or a Bermudan classic is more subtle.

SINGLE HEADSAILS

Persuading a sloop to point and foot is simple, so long as the jib luff is kept tight and the sail isn't over-sheeted. Where the luff is hanked onto the forestay, as it often is on traditional American vessels with big single jibs, luff tension shouldn't be an issue. If the sail is set flying, however, and the luff is allowed to sag, the guys in the cockpit will find themselves sheeting it ever tighter in their hopeless attempts to point up. Instead of lifting the boat to windward, the sail will be pulled around the back of the main, figuratively speaking at least, until its output is all drag and no lift. It will also backwind the main. The net results are horrid. Either by means of running backstays or by a powerful jib halyard purchase working against a suitably stiff spar, that luff absolutely must be as straight as possible.

Given that the jib is setting as it should, the secret of making good close-hauled progress in a gaffer is to bear in mind that most of them will point higher than they can actually sail. If you whack a single headsail in as though the boat were a modern racing

ABOVE: Plenty of work on the foredeck of a large classic yacht. Note the forestay is set well inboard from the stemhead

sloop, she may point up at less than 45 degrees from the true wind, but she won't be going anywhere fast. Instead, eyeball the wind ripples on the water and steer about 50 degrees off these. For a heavy vessel such as a trawler, the angle may be wider. Whatever it is, set the headsail by easing it until just before the luff lifts, then let the main off a notch. The boat will fly. Once you're making a speed approaching the square root of your waterline length in a good breeze, try nudging up towards the wind, sheeting in carefully until way starts dropping off. This is a sure sign that you're up too high; leeway increases and everything goes to hell in a basket. Keep her footing fast and all will be well.

CUTTER FORETRIANGLES

Similar essentials apply to two headsails, but there is, as one might guess, a little more to it. The secret, as before, is a tight jib luff. Without this, all else, as the preacher said, is vanity. The man of God wasn't referring to pride. What he meant was that any further efforts will be in vain, and so they will. A slack-luffed jib on a cutter inevitably ends up over-sheeted and stuffs any airstream trying to flow around the staysail. Misery results. Achieving this happy state is often all about halyard purchases, but for our current purposes we'll take it as read that there's a straight jib luff. Now we can pile on the magic.

Once the boat is making decent way, start by whacking the staysail in as hard as it will go. Sailing at around 50 degrees from the true wind, sheet the jib so that it is as close as it can come without backwinding the staysail. This may involve actually easing the jib sheet if you've hauled it in hard after tacking, because if the staysail is suffering any interference you're pointing higher than you can sail. As speed builds, the boat can often work steadily nearer the wind, bringing in the jib sheet until the staysail won't allow any more. And that's it. Hard on the breeze, going like a train.

Ideal airflow is usually best reached with the jib sheet fairlead as far outboard as possible. *Westernman's* was actually outside the bulwarks and she flew upwind like a witch on a broomstick. This permits the sail to be sheeted firmly without messing up the staysail. As the sheet hardens, the entry of the sail is flattened, allowing the boat to point higher and still foot. With the lead inboard, the jib collapses the staysail as it is sheeted and much can be lost.

On many boats, cranking up the jib halyard can actually slacken the forestay so that the staysail luff hangs out. The answer seems to be to ease the jib luff a touch until both sails adopt a similar curvature. For jib topsails, the same rules apply as for the jib, but achieving a straight luff without bending the topmast fid is a challenge to test any bosun.

Dragging the clew

Two of my early ocean cruising yachts came to me with flax canvas gaff mainsails made on England's East Coast. The smaller boat, built in Norway in 1903, had an overhanging boom. The spar on the 1911 Bristol Channel pilot cutter that replaced her ended directly above a shapely counter. Both sails had the benefits and drawbacks inherent in the material and its associated handwork. These could not be changed, but each suffered from a wicked design fault that had no business being there in the first place. The boats carried their goosenecks low down on the mast for reasons well understood by their pre-war spar makers. With tack height cast in stone, the 1970s sailmakers slipped up by pitching the clews so that, with the peak properly tensioned, neither sail's foot rose enough above the horizontal.

If you look at photographs of the great yachts racing in the Solent during the Golden Age, you'll see that when running, especially in light weather, the ends of the long main booms were sometimes perilously close to the water. These rigs were not designed for seagoing, their job was to maximise sail area. On the wind or reaching, some degree of twist lifted the booms to a more realistic angle, but for delivery passages, the hands replaced the monster mains with trysails. The giant spars were stowed on deck and substituted with shorter versions more like those favoured by working craft able to keep the sea in rough weather.

Running in a typical eight-foot ocean sea, my two mainsails were the bane of my life. As the yachts rolled, the boom ends would go under the next-door wave, dragging the sail along in a shower of solid water at anything up to nine knots and threatening horrible destruction. I could top up the boom ends, and often did, but only at the price of increased twist bringing concerns that the gaff would chafe against the upper rigging. My old friend and long-distance sailor Nick Skeates used to rig vangs on the gaff of his cutter to hold it back on a run. Fair play to him, but his boat is smaller than either of mine; a vang was just one string too many for me. Bringing in a few feet of sheet to ease the situation was another solution, but this loaded up the helm and slowed the boat.

The only real answer was to replace the sails. Penury meant that I never did this on the Norwegian. I suffered it until I sold her, and many was the night far from land that I watched, heart-in-mouth, as the fiery lights of the phosphorescence burned 20 feet outboard while we rolled along. When I finally landed some money with the bigger boat, I went to David Spargo of SKB in Falmouth for a new mainsail. We discussed the issue of the boom end and he understood straight away. He cut a sail that looked like those in my collection of original photos of working pilot cutters. Without being extreme, the boom now angled upwards from the gooseneck. It looked jaunty and I don't recall it ever dragging in the water again. Another perk was that I could control the vital twist with the sail close-hauled by heaving down on the lee quarter block. It was a great sail that turbocharged the boat for performance and did away with the ancient nightmares out on deep waters.

A sail cut to sweep up with the main boom does more than lift the eye of the observer. It makes for better performance and is more seamanlike. Such a sail gets the prize all the way, so let's have more of them!

BELOW: A beautifully designed gaff mainsail sweeps up at the clew, delighting the eye, allowing twist control and keeping the clew of the sail clear of the water on a run

Boomed staysail – friend or foe?

I must be one of the few sailors to inherit a boomed staysail, to suck it and see for a couple of years, then abandon it.

The benefits of a boom are obvious. Take the average cutter setting her jib from a bowsprit. Unless she's a full-on classic racer, the chances are she'll be short-handed for much of her life. Every time she tacks or gybes, there are more tasks than she has people to handle them. What with jib sheets, staysail sheets and running backstays, a single crew can end up hopping round the deck like a demented circus performer. Meanwhile, the helmsman is tying himself in knots trying to release runners while tripping over his shipmate. If one of these jobs can take care of itself, it's happy days.

That, in a nutshell, is the 'number one' advantage of a boom on the staysail. A carefully sheeted boom flops across the foredeck by itself, while Jack the Lad deals with the rest of the caboodle.

There's another benefit, too, that's less obvious. I once cruised in company with three-time circumnavigator Nick Skeates. Nick was sailing *Wylo II*, the gaff cutter he designed and built for himself. We were on a broad reach in a stiff tradewind that was veering round the back of an island. Nick had a boom on his staysail. I didn't. As the breeze swung aft and our staysails started to collapse, I scrambled forward to rig my booming-out pole, silently cursing the extra work as I usually do. Ten minutes later, all was secure and we were foaming along nicely with the foretriangle stabilised by the heavy spar with its topping lift and downhaul. I glanced over at *Wylo II*. Nick hadn't moved from his cockpit. He'd waited for his sail to kick across under its own initiative, then eased the sheet smartly. The sail quietly goosewinged itself, supported by its boom. Perhaps if he were going to run like this for days on end he'd have a line that secured the staysail boom. I don't know. Maybe not, but I was impressed by that classic lack of labour intensity for which all seamen must strive.

So, if you're thinking of rigging a boom for your staysail, we've found two sound reasons why you should. Why on earth would I take mine off?

The boat was a 50-foot working vessel. Photos of her on sea trials showed that 'back in the day' her staysail had been loose-footed. At some time in the intervening decades, someone decided she'd be better off with a new sail controlled by a boom. A heavy-duty iron horse appeared across the foredeck, while one of the bitts was modified to take the swivel of the spar. The sheet belayed at the forward end of the boom itself. It was a four-part tackle which ran beautifully. Because the lower block slid across the horse, when close-hauled you simply hove the sheet tight and forgot about it. The horse ensured the sail was set at the proper angle to the wind and the fact that it was there meant that the clew could be hauled down to control the twist of the sail according to wind strength. Even with no boom, East Coast smacks and Thames barges sheet their loose-footed staysails from a horse and achieve a similarly gratifying result.

Before I reveal why mine had to go despite all these advantages, there are a couple more points to be made. The first is that there are two ways to rig a boom. The one in Martyn's wonderful painting carries its 'gooseneck' on, or virtually on, the forestay. This puts some strain on the stay and means that the tension in the foot of the sail remains the same regardless of the sheeting angle. You may want to put a bit more camber into the sail as you ease the sheet and remove any rigging strains into the bargain, and this can be achieved by siting the pivot point of the boom inboard from the tack of the sail. Fittings for this vary and, as mentioned above, on my boat the pivot was sited on top of one of the bitts. On yachts with no bitts, a wooden chock robustly fastened on deck with a suitable fitting to receive the forward end of the boom serves well. Sometimes the boom even pivots from the top of the windlass. So long as the sail is set loose-footed on the boom, the leech opens as the sheet is eased, the clew rises and the sail becomes more powerful. Win-win for sure.

The first downside of the boomed staysail comes when it is dropped. Something about the geometry of the sail means that, because the clew is held aft by the boom, as the sail is lowered, the bottom end of the luff hangs up. The only way to get the sail down sweetly is to detach the lower hanks. A well-made sail gets around this by having a lacing between the luff and the hanks. This is slackened off before dropping so the lower luff can sag back from the stay. Once hoisted and tight, the lacing can be made up to assist in straightening the luff.

Why then, in light of these obvious benefits and simple solutions, did I throw all that good gear in the bin and order a new, loose-footed sail with no boom?

First up is the clutter of a boom on the foredeck, occasionally swinging around and threatening to flip luckless sailors over the side as they go about their business. Being rid of this menace is a plus.

The second and overriding answer is sail area. On my boat, as on many others, having a boom restricted the size of the sail. For the clew to pass readily across the foredeck when tacking and not murder anyone caught between the spar and the mast, the foot-length of the sail must be compromised. Getting rid of the boom allowed a small but important amount of overlap, plus some vital extra depth to the foot, both of which made a noticeable difference to performance. This was a pilot cutter with a big foretriangle that relied on a powerful staysail to drive her uphill. Essex smacks and yachts in general often differ, with smaller staysails and the jib doing most of the work. A modest staysail is then no issue. My loose-footed staysail pulled like a team of oxen and it set beautifully. I never looked back, and there was an unexpected bonus. I removed the long wrought-iron horse to clear the deck and gave it to a ship-smith pal. Ten years later he used it to make me a seven-foot iron tiller for a different boat. Waste not, want not...

RIGHT: A boomed staysail can be a good friend or a canny foe. Whether or not to specify one is a matter of personal preference, so long as the issues are thoroughly understood

CHAPTER TWO
RIGGING

For me, this will always be the heart of bosun's work. I can't think of any aspect of old-fashioned rigging that I don't enjoy, except splicing heavy wire, which I confess to leaving to the professionals if any are available.

The arrival of 1 x 19 stainless steel rigging has spelled the death knell of proper bosun work. So low have skills expectations sunk that the RYA have shamefully removed eye splicing from the Yachtmaster syllabus. Thankfully, rigging techniques and hands-on methods remain to the fore in the traditional world, where three-strand rope is everywhere, and galvanised rigging is correctly turned and seized at lower deadeyes rather than being eye-spliced and shackled to the shrouds. Shackle pins need lubrication, bowsprits demand all manner of specialised attention, purchases of varying types and powers are to be selected while vital spreader angles are decided by us alone. The list is almost literally endless.

The following articles on rigging will, I hope, delight those who know, while enlightening those who perhaps still have a way to go. I'll never forget the satisfaction I drew from working a reef cringle into the hemp bolt rope on the leech of a flax mainsail in mid-Atlantic. I was guided by the old *Admiralty Manual of Seamanship* and used only the ancient tools of my calling – a tapered hardwood fid, a mallet, a galvanised round thimble, a hefty needle, a lump of beeswax and a sailmaker's palm. It held through the next gale and I blessed the Petty Officer who told the officer what to write in the manual. You can't do that with a hi-tech sail, can you!

RATLINES

One of the many upsides to owning a classic working boat is that she won't look 'naff' rigged with ratlines. The waterfront resounds with tales of mishaps at the masthead, usually about some poor sailor who's been hoisted aloft stuck with his nose against the halyard sheave when the captive-reel winch takes a riding turn or the deckhand slopes off to the pub. Bosun's chairs or harnesses are a poor substitute for being able to nip aloft any old time without assistance.

BELOW: Experienced sailors never hold onto the ratlines going aloft. They always rely on the shrouds themselves. It only takes one seizing to carry away to spoil the day comprehensively

THE OBJECTIVE

What we're after is a set of steps in the shrouds that gets us safely from deck to hounds. On a square-rigger the ladder is extrapolated via the intermediate mastheads all the way to the base of the royal mast. For humble fore-and-afters, the hounds will do. A Bermudan-rigged yacht has less work in the rigging than her more traditional sisters, but so long as she isn't a 'gold-plater', ratlines can still look fine. For her, they serve mainly as a route upwards for a better look into a coral anchorage or finding a lead through ice. Gaffer crews often need to attend to issues above the hounds, but they have so much clutter in the way of throat cranes and peak blocks up there that onward climbing is not difficult.

The bosun's luck only runs out when he has to fettle the burgee halyard sheave or, perish the thought, re-reeve a topsail halyard after some human mistake has let go the end. Then, he must either find a volunteer to shin the pole to the topmast head or reach for his chair again. The chair is defunct without a jib topsail halyard to hoist it, so if you've been wondering whether to go for a jib top and are not great at heights, consider this: even if you don't buy the sail, the spare halyard will be worth the windage when the day comes, as come it surely will.

THE MATERIALS

As with all rope work, the sorry truth is that 'things ain't wot they used to be'. Making ratlines involves multiple eye splices. Working an eye into a length of 1½-inch manila (measured on the circumference – that's about 12 mm diameter) took only moments, with no need for any tools beyond a sharp knife and a cutting board. Tapered ends disappeared into the lay as they should, with no applications of the Zippo to persuade them to stay put. Fortunately, the rope industry now produces useful hemp and manila replicas that aren't bad to unlay even if they don't splice like natural fibre. Avoid the cheap polypropylene stuff. It's vile to tuck, rots in sunlight, and looks terrible. The plus side of modern line is that, even as small as 10 mm, which makes a neat ratline for all but the largest yachts, strength is not an issue.

The second essential for ratlines is tarred marline or a synthetic substitute. Here, progress has been made, but finding the right stuff east of the Atlantic is a tough call. The Canadians manufacture tarred nylon braidline in very small sizes that are equivalent to old-style tarred marline. 'Gangion' originates with the fishing industry and the price is right. It is superior to marline in that, being synthetic, it lasts a lot longer and is considerably stronger. Both have the vital characteristic of holding on as you pass your turns. Slippery modern line will not do this and guarantees frustration and failure. Being stretchy, gangion is even better than marline to use because as you heave on the seizings (see below), each turn binds on its predecessor for a seriously unyielding result.

Marline has worked for centuries and has the advantage of smelling even better. Gangion is good and black, it has a light tarry niff and needs no maintenance for years but, for sensual delight, you can't beat the real thing as you pile on the load and see the fresh tar come oozing out. Marline dries out after a season or so, but maybe, like me, you take pleasure in coming down the ratlines with a tar brush, enjoying the view as you freshen up the seizings in the spring sunshine.

THE METHOD

I'm sure there are many ways of attaching ropes to shrouds to make a ladder. Here's one that has served me well from the Trade winds to a damp, dripping English Channel. For shrouds in simple pairs, measure each ratline from the side of the wire closest to its neighbour. Make up the ratline by splicing an eye into each end so it fits perfectly between the shrouds without pulling them together or stretching itself. Secure each end to the shroud with a racking seizing. This means passing as many figures-of-eight between the eye and the shroud as is convenient – the biblical seven ideally – then coming back 'round and round' between each one to where you started.

Finish by passing two frapping turns round the seizing between the eye and the wire, working these into a clove hitch and whacking them up really tight, perhaps with a marline-spike as a lever. Measure up to the next ratline allowing a gap to suit your taste, and off you go again. If you are dealing with three sets of lower shrouds, the ratline is clove-hitched around the middle one.

REFINEMENT

Keep the ratlines parallel to the waterline, not the sheerline. The lowest one will probably be sited conveniently above the sheerpole. The sheerpoles are seized to the shrouds above the deadeyes or rigging screws with handy pins for hanging halyards and purchase falls.

Ratlines are notorious for pulling the shrouds together under your weight, making things tricky at the top where the wires close up. This can be scotched by inserting wooden 'ratlines', notched into the shrouds, every four or five steps, with a couple extra near the hounds.

If your boat has slippery stainless steel wire shrouds, the seizings may soon sag. Get around this by binding the shroud in way of each ratline with a turn or two of friction tape, available to the 21st-century mariner via the chandlery of the internet.

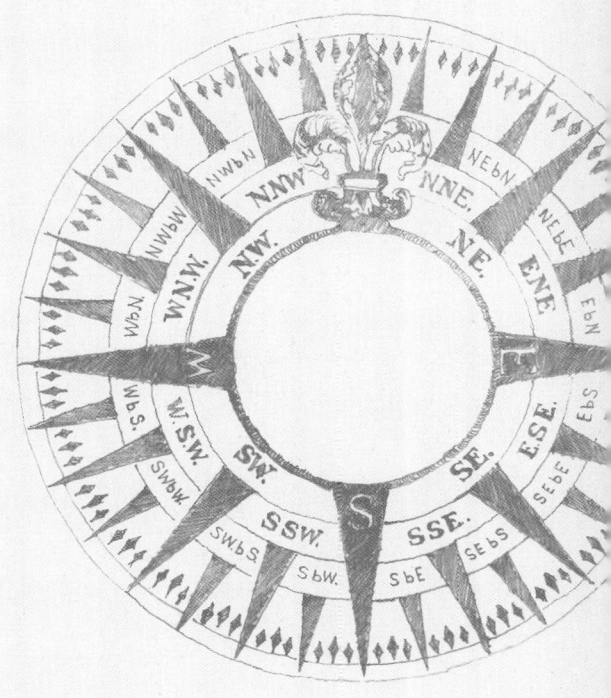

The problem of the crane

As a basic proposition, driving bolts through wooden masts is a bad idea. Taking timber out with a drill to make room for the metalwork weakens the spar by definition, and if the bolt is under any sideways strain it can worry away until water begins to get in. Because the bolt is high up the mast, this isn't salty, healthy seawater. It's the dreaded rain. Fresh water, as we all know only too well, encourages rot. Studying the work of Claud Worth from over a century ago, we find that 'back in the day' it was not unusual for a gaff-rigged mast (they were all gaff back then) to fail at the throat crane.

Readers of the Bermudan persuasion may not be aware of the throat crane, so here's what it is: the lower throat halyard block at the forward end of a gaff is invariably set back from the mast. How far depends on size and taste. The upper block on the mast in way of the hounds must be set so as to line up, otherwise it will be dragged against the spar with nasty consequences. The traditional throat crane takes care of this. It consists of a heavy bolt through the mast whose aft end carries an eye to take the hook of the upper throat block. It projects far enough at its aft side to line up vertically with the block on the gaff. Some sort of support now runs down at an angle from just forward of the eye to a plate that locates on the aft face of the mast, thus eliminating any tendency for the weight of the halyard to lever the bolt downwards. So far, so good.

Unfortunately, the bolt's problems don't end there. When squared away downwind, the eye is suffering a major sideways wrench, sometimes exacerbated by the fall of the

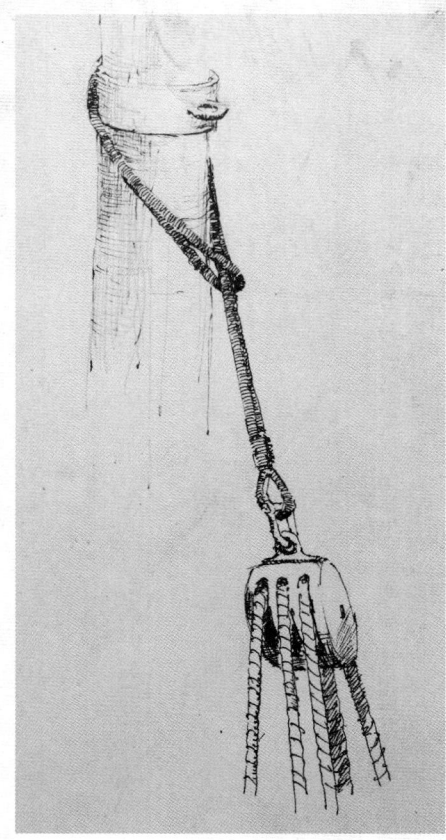

ABOVE: A stropped throat halyard block of the type favoured by the great Claud Worth moves with the throat of the gaff, as it moves from side to side with the mainsheet

peak halyard catching across the crane at the same time. The bolt is now taking a major hammering and water ingress is almost inevitable.

Back in the 1970s, I made a new mast for my 1903 Norwegian pilot cutter. The original spar had gone rotten at the hounds, almost certainly due to water ingress at the crane. I determined that my new spar should have no bolts through it and arranged what I fancied to be an inventive answer to the throat crane. I made up a wire strop, parcelled and served, that looped over the

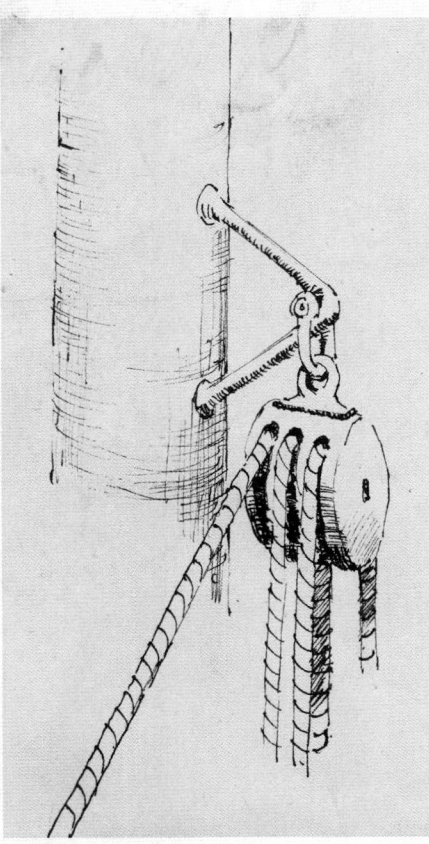

ABOVE: A well-engineered throat halyard crane works well so long as the throat of the gaff is far enough below it to allow some movement in the halyard between the blocks

masthead and rested on the hounds. The aft part of the strop was seized together with wire where a thimble formed an eye for the throat block. The strop was large enough to allow some slack between the mast and the eye. This part was gathered together aft of the mast and seized to a hefty wooden chock that held it off the mast. It was OK in theory and the strop saw me across the ocean and home again, but the chock barely lasted five minutes. The sideways wrenching mentioned above did for it in short order. What remained was not ideal, but it worked after a fashion.

When I came by my 1911 Bristol Channel pilot cutter later in life, her throat crane was a thing of beauty and functional perfection. Forged by a blacksmith who knew his business and set on the original pitch-pine mast, it did its noble work for 80 years without any issues at all. I tried to emulate it when we built *Westernman*, the 40-foot replacement, but despite our efforts, the new one was never as good. The peak halyard used to catch it, so we rigged a super-long chain link between the lower peak block and the mast to help it to drift clear, but it was never in the same league as the original.

An interesting answer to this issue comes from Claud Worth himself. In principle, it is surprisingly close to my own youthful solution, but his arrangement must have worked perfectly because he carried it on from one boat to the next.

Worth's parcelled and served flexible wire strop is considerably longer than mine and hangs from the lower peak halyard block support. His also has a seized eye with a thimble at the business end, but rather than being looped over the masthead while dressing the spar, it can be retro-fitted. The strop is passed around the spar 'double' and the thimble end rove through the bight. It is then settled down into position and, having determined where the wires crossing create a 'nip', that section is double-served. The long length of strop now 'dangling' from the peak block allows enough movement for the throat blocks to take up a healthy position relative to one another, no matter what the point of sailing. It's a pity I didn't read Claud Worth back in 1975…

MAKING SHEER POLES WORK

Every gaffer I've had any dealings with has always had sheer poles in her shrouds. Many older Bermudan yachts ship them too, and their usefulness has never been in doubt, but until now I'd never paid more than fleeting attention to the origin of the name. Admiral W H Smyth (no relation to the high-street stationer) gives us the answer in his great work on the vocabulary of the sailor, published in 1867:

'The sheer batten (sic) is a batten stretched horizontally along the shrouds and seized firmly above their dead-eyes, serving to prevent the dead-eyes from turning at that part. This is also termed a stretcher.'

My own dead-eyes have never shown any tendency to swivel out of line, so I'd assumed that the 'sheer' referred to a tendency for the shrouds themselves to twist, but it seems I was wrong. Back in the days of Italian hemp lanyards and tarred hemp shrouds, it may well be that things on the lee side sometimes became so slack that the dead-eye was able to follow a badly set-up lanyard and twist out of line.

Whatever the historical reason for the name, however, the worth of the sheer pole for clearing away the deck is inestimable. Any vessel, whatever her rig, with belaying pins along the rail in way of the chain plates has to find somewhere to stow the falls of the halyards and purchases secured there. The sheer pole is the obvious answer. When I first took over my 51-foot pilot cutter, the sheer poles were simple galvanised rods seized in place immediately above the upper dead-eyes. They supplied a convenient foothold when scrambling into the rig for a better view but were less than ideal for rope stowage. The big coils of the main halyards hung at the mast, but there was still plenty of cordage to be tidied up by the shrouds, where stout oak rails ran fore and aft inside the bulwarks, supporting a line of pins.

'Suck it and see' is a sound policy when taking on a new boat. I've learned to resist the temptation to rip in with radical improvements before I've been to sea with the previous incumbents' arrangements. Maybe they knew something I don't. In this case, they clearly didn't and I sailed to America with what amounted to a lash-up. We'd belay a purchase at deck level, coil the fall, then hank it up and hang it somehow from the pole. It all took time, especially when letting go, and it was messy.

My first task on the other side of the pond was to source four lengths of hardwood at about 3 x 1½. I offered one up to the starboard shrouds, inboard at the desired height, and marked where the wires crossed it. I did the same with a sister batten on the outboard side. Then I cut into the battens at the marks to make a slot for the shrouds and drilled through both so they could be bolted together. Tightening the bolts enabled them to nip the shrouds and stay solidly in place. A few minor adjustments to the slots with a sharp chisel and the job was done. It only remained to drill holes vertically down the

RIGHT: A well thought-out sheer pole in the shrouds provides a vital place for stowing running rigging, as well as a convenient step-up off the deck for a better view ahead

completed sheer poles to take the lengths of bronze rod I'd prepared in lieu of belaying pins, and all was sweetness on deck.

The purchase falls were still belayed down by the rail, bearing all the weight on a solid footing as before, but stowing the coils was a pleasure. Lead the first of the falls up to a pin on the new rail in the shrouds and secure it with a simple figure-eight. Coil down the rest and hang it on the pin in a seamanlike manner. They didn't do it quite like that in Admiral Smyth's Navy, but it makes a huge difference to life in a small traditional boat.

 ## HANGING THE COIL

Once the purchase fall, or the halyard, or anything else for that matter, has been securely belayed, it must be hung out of the way. By far the best procedure is the classic system used for centuries on square-riggers. Whether it's on the sheer pole of my pilot cutter or a clipper-ship's fife rail, the belay is made so that the bight comes off the pin at the top. If it's a modest line, you'll have been coiling it in hand. Make the coil so that when you offer it up to the belay, the last of the working part between coil and pin stands about nine inches from the woodwork.

If you're right-handed, hold the coil so that it hangs down from your left hand with the bitter end facing away from the pin. With your other hand, reach through the coil and grasp the bight stretched between the coil and the pin. Bring it towards you through the coil, giving it half a twist as you do. This process should draw the coil hard up against the pin. Now force the twisted bight up onto the top leg of the pin, binding the coil together with it as you jam it on. The coil is now suspended and secure. To release it, all that's needed is to flip the bight off the pin and carefully drop the coil on deck, right way up. The line runs like salt from a dry shaker. Bigger ropes are coiled on deck then lifted up to the pin, but the essential technique is identical.

THE HUMBLE BURTON

My old pilot cutter sailed with her original 1911 boom while I had her. It was 30 feet long, eight inches in diameter and was solid pitch pine. I dread to think what it weighed, and taming it was of ongoing interest. The topping lifts had no problems supporting it because the hauling end of the purchase delivered a velocity ratio of 8:1. This can be achieved without massive multi-sheaved blocks by the simple means of a burton tackle. Each of the two lifts begins at the boom end and runs aloft to the hounds to pass around a turning block. Eight feet or so below the turning block it is spliced into a single stropped 'burton block'. The rope for each burton starts in a hard eye shackled to a steel-reinforced oak pin-rail running along the bulwark stanchions inboard of the shrouds. It passes up through the burton block, then down a few feet until it terminates at the upper double-sheaved block of the final purchase. The lower purchase block is a single with a becket shackled to the pinrail, making up a 4:1 purchase rove to advantage.

The secret is that as you heave on this, the movement of the upper block is halved by the burton which acts as a 2:1 purchase in its own right. The pair multiply one another and so 8:1 can be achieved with a lot less friction than a two-block 8:1 purchase. The seven sheaves in the two blocks would generate far more frictional resistance than the four sheaves in the burton.

Burtons can be used anywhere. I've even seen them in Dyneema® as 'burton on burton on burton' to power tweakable backstays on modern race boats, but for real satisfaction you can't beat heaving up a hefty boom with lovely big elm blocks and soft three-strand rope.

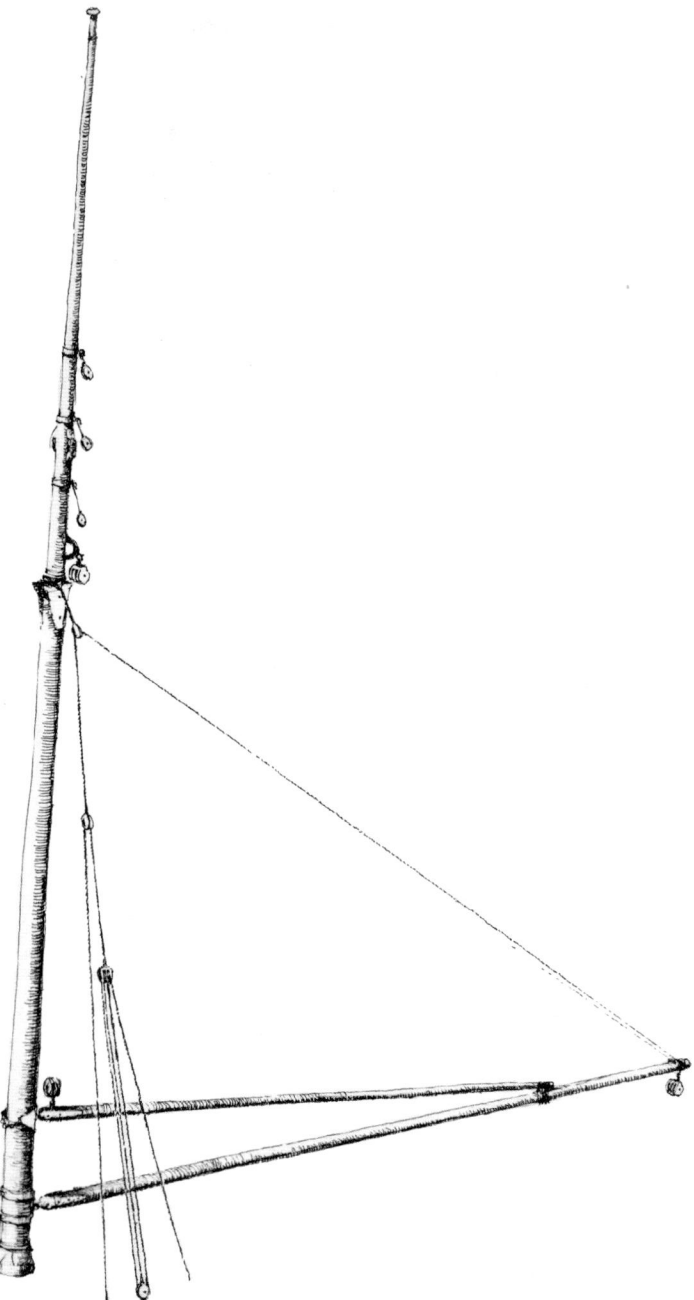

RIGHT: A four-on-two burton purchase gives 8:1 advantage with minimal friction to power the topping lift on this heavy boom

Spreaders

It's always interesting to see how older classics have managed the issue of spreaders in the shrouds. The siting of these changed radically with the arrival of Bermudan rig. Gaffers must have the full length of the mainsail luff undisturbed by fittings on the shaft of the mast so that the hoops or lacing holding it to the spar can travel freely. This means that the hounds must be far enough up not to interfere. The same, of course, goes for any spreaders needed to provide athwartships support to the upper mast.

Along with three-cornered rig came mast tracks and, ultimately, grooves in metal extrusions. Because the luff could now slide all the way to the masthead, it became possible to lower the hounds and add spreaders further down the mast to help keep the more highly stressed spar in column. Advantage was swiftly taken and by the 1930s masts looked not dissimilar to the way they do today. Gaff masts, however, constrained by luff length, could not alter significantly.

My 1911 pilot cutter came with a set of oak spreaders for the cap shrouds I still have in my shed. They angled aft from the hounds so as to offer some backstaying as well as supplying lateral support to the masthead; they ran parallel to the water. From forward, they had the look of a sorrowing pair of eyes drooping in despair. The pole mast, which was original, had no topmast and was unambitious in length. I had crossed and recrossed the Atlantic with it before I found an old photo of similar boats in Barry Harbour from around 1905. None of them had spreaders. I promptly took them down and never looked back. The mast was as stout as ever and I cruised the boat a further ten years in trouble-free security.

If you have a topmast, you will need spreaders for sure, but if you don't, think hard about whether they would have been there in the boat's early days. They may have been fitted by well-meaning yachtsmen who had seen them on other craft and imagined they would be an improvement. It's a natural post-Bermudan knee-jerk reaction.

As to the form of spreaders on gaffers, there are as many as there are boats. Often, a round-section iron bar runs out from the hounds, mounted on a swivelling bolt with some sort of fitting at the outboard end to take the shroud. The swivel manages one of the over-riding problems of gaff rig, which is that when the boom is squared away enough to take out weather helm on a run or reach, the gaff is trying to pivot forward of square. This is bad news, but if the lee spreader can swing out of the way, it helps a lot.

One form of fixed spreader I admired so much that I copied it for a new boat of my own is seen on *Jolie Brise*, the 55-ton Le Havre pilot cutter-cum racing yacht. Her spreaders are like an open framework. Each one has two main members running out from the hounds. At their inboard ends they are as far apart as the mast's diameter. They come together outboard and have one or two crosspieces on the way to support and strengthen them. In a seaway they are rock solid, giving a skipper a lot of confidence

LEFT: Because she has a topmast, this yacht's mast must have spreaders, but a glance aloft shows how awkward they can make life

in his topmast. The space between the members offers an instant fair lead to some of the halyards and general cordage running down from aloft, keeping it clear of chafe from the gaff. Altogether an excellent idea, dating perhaps from the great E G Martin, or possibly even the pilots themselves back in 1913. We may never know, but whoever it was got it right.

Many of us are simply stuck with the spreaders we have. Often, these work well enough and little can be done to improve them, but much can be achieved by attending to the slant they make with the horizontal. To be fully effective, spreaders should bisect the angle they create in the cap shroud. If rigged correctly they will therefore sweep up from the hounds to the shroud. By happy chance, the result is invariably pleasing to the eye. Spreaders that poke out parallel to the water neither look good, nor do they function as well as they could. Drooping spreaders are an abomination, dragging the eye down with them to the depths of visual degradation.

On a more practical level, wooden spreaders take a major beating from the sun. Varnish is all fine and dandy for the bits you can see, but only the seagulls get to admire the top. I always painted mine white or cream to reflect the heat. Worked like a charm.

LEFT: Martyn has given us this masthead man to exemplify the ecstasy of the sailor's freedom. On the technical side, the spreaders offer creative options for leading difficult lines and standing rigging

BAGGYWRINKLE

You don't see baggywrinkle as much as you used to. If you aren't familiar with the term, it's those fluffy cylindrical pads that guard against chafe up in the rigs of salty vessels. Time was when any self-respecting gaffer had a few lengths on the runners or the topping lifts to protect the mainsail going downwind. The bosuns of square-riggers clapped it onto their forestays under the hounds to save their course sails from oblivion. For ocean cruisers it was once a rite of passage. Today, it's a rarity. I wonder why?

Chafe still goes on in traditional craft. In some ways, it's worse than it used to be because, with modern sailcloth, the stitching stands proud and is victim to anything with a fancy to rub away at it. On canvas, the stitches bedded in, so only the cloth was vulnerable. I suspect that the reason is a rising awareness about windage. A single spare halyard of half-inch diameter on a 50-foot mast has a cross-sectional area of four square feet. Three of these are the equivalent of a small toilet door. Try holding that open against force six when you're hacking to windward and you'll see why keeping the rig as clean as possible is important. A one-foot length of baggywrinkle at four inches diameter costs us a significant 48 square inches, but it doesn't do to get too fussy about windage. In many cases, a few strips of baggywrinkle provide a fair trade-off against this obvious downside by neutralising known chafe spots. So, how are we to make and rig it?

Here's where the progress forced upon us by synthetic fibres represents a genuine improvement. I've made yards of baggywrinkle using organic materials. It was a lovely job and it smelt divine, but after a season or two my efforts would unravel in their place aloft and bring shame upon the ship until I girded up my loins and dealt with it. Today, the stuff should last as long as we do ourselves. Traditionally, the core of baggywrinkle was tarred, two-strand marline. Now, of course, you can use some sort of polyester marline substitute. Most of these are not nearly so enjoyable to work with, but if you can lay hold of some Canadian fishing-boat gangion, it offers a fair substitute that will outlast any of God's creatures that walk on two legs. As for the fluff, this is supplied by worn-out rope, originally hemp, manila or sisal too tired for any other purpose. In a polyester world, any three-strand will do, except the dreaded polypropylene. This is a truly nasty product that will soon start to shed bits and pieces all over the deck as the sun degrades it. It's rough to touch too, so is counter-productive at the business end of the job.

To make a useful pad for any boat between 20 and 50 feet, first take a fathom of marline, double it and knot the ends together. Stretch it out tight between two suitable fixtures at about waist height. The height is important as it enables you to work standing up straight and thus you will not tire your back for leaning on the bar at the end of the day. Now pick up your useless old rope. Measure it off into something like 8-inch lengths and cut it up. These come apart easily into strands. Unravel the strands into smaller units and tease them out so that the fibres are no longer twisted. Cow-hitch these into the doubled-up marline and pull tight. Leave a short length of marline at each end for tying off in the rigging. When the marline is full, the job is done. It only remains to deploy the fruits of your labours.

Swing aloft in the bosun's chair and site yourself beside the rope to be baggywrinkled. Clove hitch one end of the marline to the rope, then wind the whole shooting match snugly round and round until you get to the marline at the other end. You may find you have to twist the baggywrinkle here and there to keep the yarns of old rope pointing outwards. Tie off the marline and that's it. If you need a bigger pad, just make it longer.

RIGHT: Passing fresh baggywrinkle on a sunny day

MAST RAKE AND BOOM ANGLE

Mast rake is one of those critical areas where aesthetics balance pragmatism. It can vary between such extremes as the mid-19th-century American pilot schooner with very little backstaying but enormous rake to make up for it, and an Essex smack's topmast bowsed forward in anticipation of lots of topsail sheet to pull it back into column. Too much aft slant can generate weather helm. In practice, however, a boat is tossed around so much at sea that, so long as rake is kept within reason, other considerations may prove equally important.

How much rake any original boat needs is best discovered by examining old photographs. A useful example is the pole-masted Bristol Channel pilot cutter. She carries no backstays. Instead, she has 'swifters' that run from abaft the lower shrouds up to the jib halyard blocks. These give the stick all the support it needs and allow the jib luff to be set up drum-tight against them. For the arrangement to work, the mast must have some rake so as to open up the angles aloft. Without it, support disappears, the setup doesn't function and dismasting can be the result. If the rake is right, the rig is rock-solid and you get a great-looking boat as a spin-off.

BOOM ANGLE

Traditional rigs invariably had mainsails cut so that the boom was well down at the gooseneck, sweeping up to the clew. For a yacht with low freeboard, this not only pleases the eye, it stops the sail from rolling into the water downwind and allows extra scope for heaving down on the clew when close-hauled to control twist in a sail with no kicker or permanent vang. Anyone more worried about health and safety than style and performance will stuff the boom way up and parallel to the water like the wretched apologies seen on white charter boats. Too many craft are spoiled like this nowadays, sailing around with the main sagging like a barn door with the top hinge off. Time was when any sailmaker supplying such a horror would have been clapped in the town stocks so that every urchin who knew what a boat was meant to look like could pelt him with the leftovers of Sunday lunch.

RIGHT: Pitching the boom angle correctly is a tricky art. Too little rise can kill the look of the sheerline below it. It will also end up dragging the boom in the water off the wind. Too much makes it look impossibly jaunty and steals sail area

Boom Angle.   Martyn R. Mackrill.

SETTING UP DEADEYES: THE EXCELLENT AND THE LUDICROUS

A proper deadeye is reliable, functional and a delight to use. A badly designed imitation carries a maker's guarantee of disappointment. Here's how to spot one: beware of tiny rope holes in a big, flat disc of wood. This wretched artefact has been produced by someone who has looked up the strength of modern cordage on a website but failed to realise that there's more to it than that. Very often these deadeyes are made from cheap wood which is another giveaway. If the grain is running fore and aft rather than up and down or round and round, it's asking to end up as a case of 'tear along the dotted line'. Stands to reason, doesn't it, yet they're available for cash money.

A decent deadeye is thick and has three big holes. It often carries a light, decorative score-line around the face outside the lanyard holes to show that makers care about its appearance, as well they should. The holes will be wider than the lanyards and well chamfered, ideally with the chamfers 'meeting' in the middle of the hole so that the rope can render easily. One hole in the upper deadeye of each pair will bear no chamfer on one side, to take the stopper knot on the lanyard end.

The wood will be lignum vitae. It usually blackens once it has kicked around the oceans for a few decades, with no discernible grain unless the unit has been cut from the heart of the log with the grain running around it. Looks right and is right.

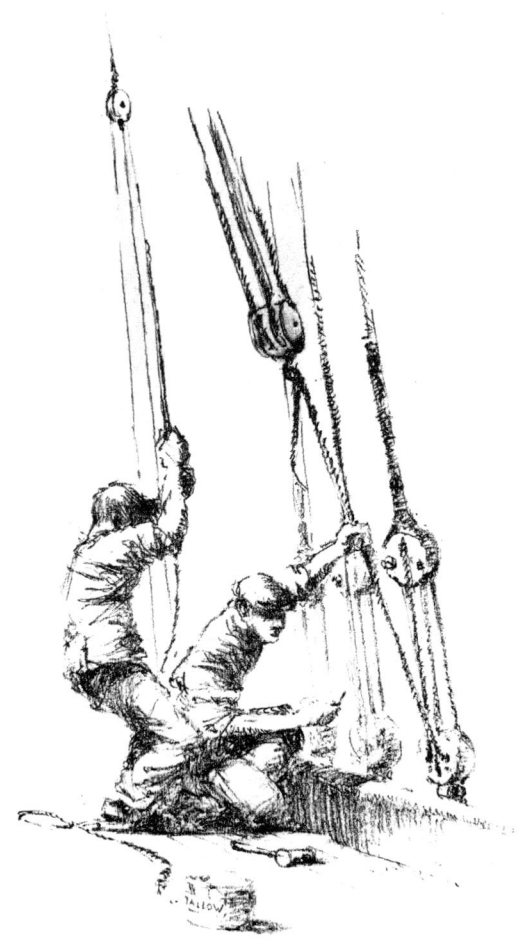

ABOVE: Setting up dead-eyes is an ancient skill – and very satisfying it is too

SET 'EM UP JOE

It's always easy for me to remember which side of the upper deadeye takes the stopper knot. My pilot cutter had two head compartments. The port head was aft, the starboard was forward and since they weren't up on deck, they were sited inboard. The stopper knots went with the loos: 'port aft, starboard forward, and inside on both sides'.

Once the end is made up like this, reeving the lanyards is easy and turning a three-strand lanyard anticlockwise against its natural inclination is impossible. The holes are well greased with tallow, widely available on the internet. With the lanyards rove and tallowed, all that remains is to tension up, starting with the shroud whose loop is lowest on the pile at the hounds. It's easy on my boats because the throat halyards always carry a purchase on the standing end, giving 16:1 on the final heave. If you don't have this benefit, perhaps you should look to it, but in lieu you can always rig a roving purchase on the hauling end. A soft mallet helps the lanyard to render. Pile on a load of grunt, secure the halyard, then whack the parts of the lanyard to encourage it to slither through the holes.

Now, here's the clever bit. Received wisdom is that once the lanyard is set up, the bight of the working end should be seized to the adjacent part two or three times. This will hold it in place while you cow-hitch the end to the shroud above the upper deadeye. Forty years ago, an elderly Norwegian lady rigger told me this is both tedious and unnecessary. All you need is a small hardwood wedge, fashioned with a gouge so that it slips between the last part of the lanyard and its hole in the deadeye. Tap it into the hole with the mallet, then ease off on the halyard. You'll see it pull in and lock. Now make your cow hitch, then wriggle the wedge out and move on to the next shroud.

The benefit is obvious. By the time you arrive at the last shroud, you will almost certainly want to adjust the earlier ones to even things up. If you've made three racking seizings on each one you aren't going to be too happy. This way, you just whip off the cow hitch and do what's needed. When the whole rig is to your satisfaction, seize the tails of the lanyards to their neighbours and that's the job. I can set up the rig on a pilot cutter singlehanded in a couple of relaxed hours like this, and a delightful afternoon it makes.

HOUSING BOWSPRITS

If you sail a yacht with a short bowsprit, the spar may well be a permanent fixture. The classic cutter with working craft origins, however, can usually bring her bowsprit inboard. Not only does this shorten the vessel for docking purposes, it also outsmarts the harbourmaster in times when we are no longer charged simply for that part of the boat in which we can live. On small vessels

BELOW: Every boat has her own system for housing the bowsprit, but it must work easily

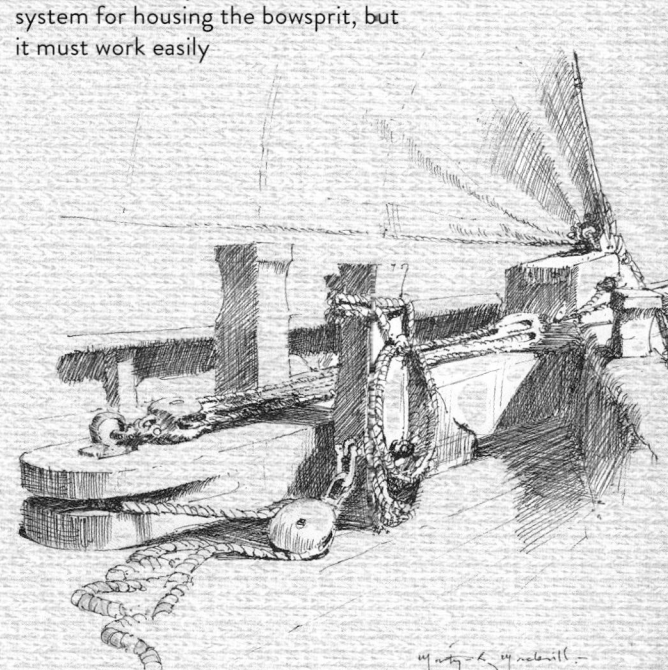

it's sometimes enough just to grab the spar and shove it out, but as boats grow larger, this becomes impractical and, unless you have a Dutch or Thames barge arrangement to steeve it up, a system must be devised. Here are some options:

A SIMPLE HANDLE

I was impressed when sailing on the original 35-foot Colin Archer *Velsia* to see her owner, the West Country surveyor David Cox, run out his bowsprit using a neat wooden handle at the upper inboard end. Such was the balance of the system that, with the bobstay slacked away, the spar seemed to fly out with no effort at all. It was housed equally easily. No doubt the gammon iron was tallowed to assist, but I've never found anything easier.

A HEEL ROPE

Probably the best arrangement with a bigger spar is to use a heel rope. This works well with an offset spar running between foredeck bitts. On a medium-sized boat, a 'dumb sheave' is cut athwartships into the aft end of the spar. This can be greased with tallow if need be to help the rope render. The spar is measured so that a foot or more is left aft of the bitts when it is fully run out. The heel rope is dead-ended on the aft face of one bitt at the same height as the fid that retains the bowsprit when run out. The other bitt carries a snatch block. The bight of the rope is passed around the dumb sheave and the hauling end comes away aft from the snatch block to a convenient spot for the crew to tail on. The end of the spar, complete with cranse iron and all its gear, must be outside the tallow-lubed gammon iron before any hauling begins. The fall can even be led to a winch if the hands are grumbling. Someone may have to support the spar 'up and down' until it is fidded, but so long as the bobstay, the topmast forestay and any bowsprit shrouds are let off, the operation will pass readily enough.

A MORE SOPHISTICATED HEEL ROPE

I once skippered a Brixham Trawler with a magnificent bowsprit arrangement which had a notable refinement of the heel rope described above. The spar itself was of square section in its after part and instead of a dumb sheave, it carried a full patent sheave at its inboard end. The heel rope ran round this like silk. The reason for the flat surfaces was that instead of having one of the hands bear down on the spar to keep it from dipping as it ran out, the bitts carried rollers top and bottom which retained the bowsprit and on which it ran without friction. When it was out, the fid was popped in and the bobstay set up to ram it into position. Beautiful.

BOWSPRIT TRICING LINES

I suppose I've been lucky. All my traditional yachts have been cutter-rigged with running bowsprits. This means that when confronted by harbourmasters demanding money with menaces calculated on what I call my 'sparred length', I can always pull in the sprit and confound the blighters. Apart from the occasional kind-hearted berthing master prepared to turn a blind eye, which includes every French official I have ever come across – sportsmen all – the idea of charging only for the bit of boat I can actually live in simply doesn't cross their avaricious minds.

A second advantage of the running bowsprit is that, because the boat is a true cutter with her mast supported by a forestay at the stemhead, I don't need to carry a bobstay when no jib is set. If the bobstay isn't helping to keep the mast up, it becomes superfluous at anchor or when moored. Fixed bobstays are a menace in these circumstances, keeping us awake when the cable graunches across a taut bobstay wire. Inappropriate plastic pipe is sometimes employed to offset the damage, but it's a pig in a poke. The proper answer is to use chain for the bobstay, set it up with a powerful tackle led to the foredeck, then rig a tricing line halfway along the chain to heave it up when it isn't wanted.

On my 32-footer I had a 4:1 purchase between the upper end of the bobstay chain and the bowsprit's cranse iron. The fall led inboard. After anchoring, the first job was to let this off and pull up on the tricing line. Bobstay gone, peace rules. With bigger boats, including a 35-ton pilot cutter, I have used chain from the waterline, set up by a wire tackle rove to disadvantage at 2:1, led inboard to a 4:1 tackle, giving me 8:1 in all. When the 4:1 was hauled right in, there were only inches between the blocks, so no stretch worth the name spoiled the effect.

More recently, Dyneema® core took the place of the wire. It looks fine without the coat and it doesn't rust. Either way, the 2:1 tackle had minimal stretch. Who needs a bottle screw with a set-up like that?! The only downside is when the fall of the 2:1 is slacked away, the eye in the end that hooks to the 4:1 will flip out of reach. A simple, lightweight messenger line solves this. A quiet night is guaranteed while the tricing line works its magic, and having a tackle rather than a rigging screw on the bobstay will make defeating the harbourmaster so much easier next time he fingers his tape measure.

TOPMAST FORESTAY

With the bobstay dealt with, the second source of grief for running out is often a pre-measured topmast forestay. Many pole-masted working boats that didn't set jib topsails had no outer forestay at all. If they did, like any boat with a topmast, they would opt for a running stay. If this is the choice, the wire is led through a block on the upper lug of the cranse iron, then inboard along the bowsprit. It ends in a hard eye with thimble, to which is hooked a 4:1 tackle inboard of the stem head. The aft block of this can be secured to the bitts or any other convenient place, and the hauling end made off on its own cleat or pin. The arrangement has a further advantage in that the whole stay can be brought inboard to hank on a jib-topsail, then sent back out again to hoist it.

STAYING AN OFFSET BOWSPRIT

There is much to be said for a working-boat style offset bowsprit, especially when the spar is to be reefed or run in, but it comes with an inherent drawback. The bowsprit shroud on the same side of the boat as the spar will be operating at a disadvantage. If the outer end of the spar is lined up to put the cranse iron on the centreline rather than parallel to the fore-and-aft line as it might well be, the angles are even worse. The result is often a bowsprit that is strongly rigged on one side and weak on the other. One of my boats suffered this and the late Ed Burnett found the answer in T Harrison Butler's written works. We made up a single spreader or 'whisker' for the weak side. A simple ring bracket on the deck's covering board meshed with a ring at its heel. The outboard end carried a curved T-shaped fitting with a concave outer surface of the type usually seen on gaff spans. We shoved the whisker out so that the T fitting located in the shroud, then kicked it round to the optimum angle. The compression held it in place. For long trips, we'd seize it to be sure. When it was going to be in the way coming alongside, a hefty boot dislodged it and away it went with a clatter, hanging meekly down from its bracket. What a difference it made.

DYARCHY FORESTAY

I was recently speaking with an old friend who is restoring a Fife-built yacht from the 1930s. As work on the hull was nearing completion he was thinking about rigging. He is, as one might say, approaching seniority in years and was unwilling to set his working jib flying as per Mr Fife's original specification. The reasons will be obvious to anyone who has had the experience. The possible solution of a Wykeham Martin furling gear had been set aside for aesthetic reasons. It wouldn't look quite right with the yacht at rest, he felt and, like many of us, he had suffered varying results with these gears.

As we discussed his problem we recalled that the great English designer Jack Laurent Giles had come up with a different answer for his famous 45-foot cruising gaff cutter Dyarchy. This masterpiece of innovation was built in 1939 for Mr Roger Pinckney, vice-commodore of the Royal Cruising Club, to replace his previous yacht, a Bristol Channel pilot cutter of the same name. Pinckney knew his stuff, and together with Giles came up with a solution to this perennial problem which has stood the test of time. It incorporates the handling advantages of hanking a bowsprit jib onto a stay with the benefit of being able to do the whole job while safely inboard on deck.

The jib-stay is of flexible wire. It dead-ends up the mast in the immediate vicinity of the jib halyard blocks, either stropped round the spar with a leathered soft eye, or shackled to a tang via a hard eye. From there it leads down to a turning block rigged fore and aft at deck level. This can be either shackled to the cranse iron if the bowsprit is very short, or hooked to a traditional traveller if the wire will be out of reach from the deck when set up. After passing through the turning block, the stay is finished off with a hard-eye. The clever bit is that, at rest, the jib stay is under no tension at all, so the bight above the block can be grabbed and held in hand. The jib tack is shackled to the eye and the luff is hanked to the floppy standing part which is comfortably within reach. The halyard is shackled to the head of the jib and the traveller sent out to the bowsprit end.

When the sail is hoisted the hanks slide up the jib-stay and as the halyard is tensioned the luff of the sail transfers the pull to the tack, thence to the stay itself, which tightens up magically around the turning block. The wire then acts as an extra forestay, strengthening the mast, and giving the luff of the sail a far better chance of standing straight than any jib halyard purchase can do with a flying sail. If there's no winch, of course, there's no law against having a halyard purchase on the other end of the one or two-part halyard because, as we all know, any attempt to persuade a yacht to sail to windward with a soggy jib luff is doomed to disappointment.

As the sail is lowered with this arrangement, it remains under control at all times. When the halyard tension comes off, the standing part of the wire is allowed to sag inboard with the sail still hanked on to it. Let fly the traveller and the whole shooting match is safe in hand. The task is far less fraught with potential horrors than when a decent-sized flying jib is set or handed on a breezy day.

This system has been used on a number of well-found boats in recent years, including the fabulously slippery gaff cutter *Zinnia*, designed by the late Ed Burnett for Ian and Sue Pople of Keyhaven. Like Roger Pinckney, Ian Pople (also RCC) knows more than most of us about how to make a boat go.

ABOVE: The Dyarchy forestay perfected by Jack Laurent Giles and Roger Pinckney for the 45-foot cutter of the same name, offers an effective alternative to chancing your luck with a jib set completely flying

He and Sue sailed *Zinnia* from the English Channel to the Caribbean and back with no engine, no heads and no holes in the hull at all. She absolutely flew and Ian reported that changing jibs on a dark night was a relatively seamless process.

My pal with the Fife plans to follow suit. He won't be sorry.

THINKING BEYOND THE BOX

Messrs Giles and Pinckney's idea also provides as good an answer as I've seen to the vexed question of tensioning the luff of a gaff topsail while keeping it under control. On a large vessel with the sail permanently bent to the topmast using hoops this is no special problem. It's the majority of sails hoisted from the deck that cause head-scratching, which is where the *Dyarchy* forestay system comes in. Here's the spec:

Use suitably traditional-looking, light-weight, stretch-free Dyneema® for the leader. Wire is unwieldy here, causes chafe and wrecks varnish. Nobody will notice and the results are a joy. Strop this around the mast at the upper mast band or some other high point that will stop it sliding down – perhaps the top peak block. Bring it to the deck outside everything and pass it through a turning block. The free end can be much longer than on the *Dyarchy* forestay. When the load is off, this allows the bight of the leader to sag a long way from the mast, making it easy to hank on the sail. A tackle is permanently rigged with its lower block on the free end of the leader. The upper block is hitched to the topsail downhaul and you're ready to hoist in the usual way with halyard and sheet. Masthead the halyard and belay, take up some slack on the sheet, then heave down hard on the tackle. This pulls the leader tight like magic while tensioning the luff of the sail. When the time comes to drop, ease off the tackle, surge away on the halyard and sheet, then smile as the hanked-on sail comes down under perfect control on its now-slack leader.

MAINSHEET ARRANGEMENTS

Not long ago, I found myself sailing aboard a new yacht, clearly built to a price. Instead of a mainsheet traveller, she had a length of skinny Dyneema® with an eye worked into the middle to which the lower mainsheet block was attached. Without a traveller – today's equivalent of the classical 'horse' – no modern Bermudan sloop can be sailed properly upwind in light airs or, some might say, in any airs at all. This vital piece of gear allows the sheet to take its part in controlling mainsail twist by assisting the vang as it tensions the leech. Classics that predate the 1950s generally don't have a permanently rigged vang, so the only downward component on the leech of the mainsail comes from the sheet. How this is rigged has a marked effect on the downward force that can realistically be applied, and over the years three methods have evolved. Luggers and loose-footed mainsails are a

RIGHT: Mainsheet blocks hung from wire spans like this are common on larger classic yachts. The system spreads the load away from a single attachment point

different proposition, but anything with a main boom will, in all probability, use one of the systems described below to shape the main without killing the boat:

THE SINGLE ATTACHMENT POINT

This is the poor relation of mainsheet arrangements. Because it makes no attempt to spread the load of the sheet through a number of attachment points, it is usually favoured by smaller craft, although it can be seen on big working boats with no pretensions to sparkling windward performance. One block is sited at the boom end and a second is shackled to a central fixed deck fitting. It's simple and effective, but it has one big problem.

Whether gaff or Bermudan, most classics don't sail well to windward with the mainsheet hove in hard amidships. This might assist in pointing high, but the boat slows down so much that any gains are lost in diminished speed. The sheet must therefore be eased off the centreline. As soon as the boom moves outboard from the deck block, the end rises and twist compromises the set of the sail, particularly when a gaff topsail is set. Some degree of control can be achieved by using a quarter tackle, but the arrangement is never ideal. If it's what you have, you've little choice but to live with it and be aware.

When it comes to hulls with long straight keels such as fishing trawlers, the losses are nothing like so apparent as in livelier craft. These hefty vessels are never going to point like yachts whatever they set in the way of sails, so choosing this layout gives them an economic solution with little real performance lost along the way. Their secret is to crack off, let her go, and make up for lost pointing by enjoying the straight-line speed delivered by that long waterline.

THE 'SNUBBER AND QUARTER-BLOCK' SOLUTION

The answer for most medium and large-sized yachts whose underwater shape encourages lively close-hauled performance is a short midships horse and a pair of quarter blocks with either a triple block on the boom, or a set of singles mounted on spans. The first of these arrangements is also often favoured by pilot cutters. The two vertical supports of the horse are carried down through the deck and bolted underneath, sometimes clear through the stern chock. A double block sits in the centre of the horse, with rubber buffers on either side to take the snatch of a gybe or the snubbing of a heavy boom in light airs. My own 35-ton 1911 pilot cutter had no rubber. Instead, she featured a heavy spring which compressed as the two stirrups holding the block were pulled inward by the boom as it snubbed. It worked beautifully.

The quarter blocks are also securely mounted, so the upward pull of the sheet is distributed over four points, all through-bolted, which renders it virtually bullet-proof. The sheet is, of course, double-ended, which means two people can readily heave it in together if they are strong enough, one on each end. When sheeting in from a broad reach, one crew can grab the sheet on its downward leg from the boom block to the weather quarter block, while a mate takes hold of the tail 'beyond the block' as it were. They can then pull rhythmically together standing in good positions to give it all they have.

When the boom is just off the centreline in a close-hauled attitude, some degree of leech tension can be achieved by hardening up on the lee quarter block. This will pull the boom down without trying very hard to centre it because the block is sited directly underneath.

THE FULL-WIDTH MAINSHEET HORSE

Historically, many types of boat used full or part-width mainsheet horses. This divides the load into two places while giving the crews a clear pull to heave down on the close-hauled mainsail leech. Colin Archer's pilot cutters had full-width horses of wrought iron bolted to stout quarter-posts. My daughter's 28-foot Falmouth Quay Punt built by Harley Mead in 1909 has her original half-width horse, and she goes upwind like a train. Our artist, Martyn Mackrill, has just fitted a three-quarter-width bronze horse onto the Fife he is restoring for his own use. Martyn's will be rigged with quarter blocks for the best of both worlds, but the working craft are often rigged 'in the raw' with no quarter blocks. The lower sheet block slides across to the lee side for close-hauled sailing and the sheet is hove down carefully to give the desired sail shape. The only drawback is that the fall of the sheet often comes off the top block and is belayed on the extended pin of the bottom one, so as not to pull the lower block away from its natural position. The process can be awkward, but the sail is smiling all the way. As has been irrefutably observed, 'Only God is perfect.'

By the way, Falmouth working boats, those doyens of traditional sailing performance, use a full-width horse rigged like a modern traveller. Says it all, doesn't it?

TOPPING LIFT
ONE LIFT OR TWO?

For reasons of pragmatic convenience, most of us are stuck with the topping lift arrangements we inherit. That being said, the advantages of having twin lifts, one either side, are inestimable. At sea, a boat is rarely, if ever, head to wind for sail-handling manoeuvres unless she relies on her engine. It follows that, half the time, a single topping lift will be to leeward, cutting into the bunt of the mainsail when set up. Nasty for Bermudan yachts, horrible on gaffers. If you've a pair, the weather one is always used for reefing. It can also take the weight of the boom in light going, adding a degree of twist to an otherwise dead-flat rig with the life dragged out of it by the weight of the boom. Twin topping lifts are winners all ends up. When slung from strops carrying the blocks just below the hounds they sit well out of the way and the only downside is perhaps a little extra weight aloft. Compared with the benefits, do we really care?

LAZY JACKS

Time was when these were clumsy lines spliced into the topping lifts and passed beneath the boom. They helped to control the sail, but they were always messy. Today, we can tame our mains successfully using tastefully chosen modern line. Two single blocks are seized aloft in a convenient place, usually an aft shroud. The 'jacks' start with their own lightweight halyard somewhere near the gooseneck, passing up through the blocks and down to a pair of thimbles well below them. Further light lines run through these with secondary thimbles seized on either end. The four working parts now pass through these secondaries down to small, evenly spaced eyelets screwed to the boom under the foot of the sail, then back up to the other side. It pays to seize their mid-points to the eyelets. Properly thought out, they will hold the lowered sail tidily to await a permanent stow.

If they are in the way when you're on show or sailing, ease the halyard, grab the bights of the jacks and pull them forward. Hook them onto something and set up the halyard. They disappear along the boom.

There's only one snag. To stow the sail inside lazy jacks, you've little choice but to flake it.

ARTIFICIAL HEMP

Nothing sets off a classic yacht or workboat like her ropes. Modern cordage is so much better than anything produced by Mother Nature, even when ably assisted by HM Dockyards' ropewalks, that unless we are reproducing a very old vessel as authentically as humanly possible, not to use it is hard to justify. In the early days of polyester cordage, the trouble was that it just didn't make the grade for appearance, but that is history. Hemp and manila lookalikes have been around for decades, thank goodness. The only question remaining is which ones to choose.

Anything based on polypropylene fibres should be given the widest of berths. It looks cheap and nasty, it isn't over-strong and it degrades in sunlight like a copper coin in a glass of Coca-Cola. When it comes to the good stuff, I'm old enough to remember the better qualities of 'real' rope. Manila, in particular, was a joy to splice. Some of today's softer equivalents are the same. Others are laid up so tightly that you need tools to get stuck into the lay. These variants feel harder and don't coil or knot so happily either. While possibly more stretch-resistant, they just aren't so nice to work with.

Perhaps I'm being fussy. They're all far stronger than the originals, so why not find one that's friendly in your hands and rejoice.

RIGHT: The late Peter Martin, who originally rigged the 19-metre cutter *Mariquita* specified low-stretch braid-on-braid halyards finished in buff

CHAPTER THREE
WORKING THE SHIP

Seamanship and working the ship are subjects with a considerable amount of cross-over. Reefing a mainsail could sit comfortably in the other section, as might steering with tiller lines and stowing a staysail so that it looks like a piece of sculpture, but that is the strength of what we do. You can't always break our art down into neat little packages. One thing floods over into another, so that the complete bosun is the person who understands them all and moves, seemingly weightlessly, from one to another. Students studying for a Day Skipper qualification in night school or on distance-learning systems can take in every single item of knowledge that those who set the syllabus have decided they need, but it is only when they go to sea with a wise instructor that they begin to understand that success lies not so much in knowing everything, but in deciding which part of the knowledge to deploy for a given situation.

Working the ship's a bit like that. Some of what follows is about equipment such as mast hoops, or guard rails with stanchions, and how such things can make life easier. Other nuggets are concerned with how to throw your body weight at a rope rather than just trying to pull it, or how to transfer a heavily loaded line from the hands of half a dozen people hanging onto it, onto a pin without losing an inch of slack. Working the ship successfully is a bit like seamanship really. The trick is to manage all these things without anyone noticing you've done it.

RIGHT: This owner, and his professional hands, have everything set to a nicety so that the yacht is surging ahead with no apparent effort. It's all in the attention to detail

THE OLD-FASHIONED LIZARD

Have you ever noticed how a jib topsail sheet never quite seems to lead as you'd like it to? These lethal ropes generally pass outside everything on their whippy way down and aft from the clew of that powerhouse up in the sky. I've sailed on a number of quite large vessels where the sheet is never properly tamed and ends up as an uncontrolled 'live' rope with some optimist hanging onto it trying to jam it onto a cavel or a cleat after a tack. If he's skilled or lucky he'll contrive to snatch a turn before the sail really takes the wind. Otherwise he's either a rope-burn casualty or, if fear of the mate prevents him from letting go of a hopeless case, he's carried away over the side.

The answer to this is, of course, to lead the sheet through a turning block. A couple of useful hands the right side of a block on deck are in with a reasonable chance of a result in comparative safety. On a windy day when they can't quite manage to heave it snug, the bosun can swing by with a handy billy to crank in the rest on a 4:1.

If you're really in the money, the turning block will be perfectly sited to apply the right proportion of the sheet tension to the leech and the foot of the sail, but in my experience this is rarely the case, especially when the same turning block has to serve 'jib-tops' of two different sizes. A true jib-top rarely has its clew pitched at the same height as a near-full-hoist Yankee, yet the block often has to lead the sheets of both. A Yankee will usually have a lower clew and the sheet will be putting too much heave-ho on the foot of the sail while letting the leech hang out for better weather, spilling wind in the process. What's needed to get around this are the services of a 'lizard' which a good bosun will have, if not about his person, at least tucked away ready in his bag.

A lizard is simply a traditional bullseye with a length of rope spliced tightly around it. A modern cruising yacht will sort out a bit more downward pull from the headsail sheet by sliding the fairlead car forward on its track. The same effect can be achieved with a lot less drama by slipping the bullseye of a lizard onto the bight (middle) of the sheet, then heaving down on its rope and making it fast on some useful point. Anything will do, a cavel, a cleat, a belaying pin or even a stanchion base. The position isn't critical, because the lead is adjusted by the downward pull, not by how far forward or aft it is.

Now that I have retired from day-to-day sailing in gaff cutters, I still use lizards on my 1980s 'classic' Bermudan yacht. Like all of her type, and many a fine wooden yacht these days as well, when I crank half a dozen rolls into the genoa in a stiff breeze, the lead position needs adjustment. I have a track for this. It runs outboard along the capping rail, but it doesn't have the useful tackle permanently rigged for adjusting it as is found on modern quality craft such as the offerings of Hallberg-Rassy or 'Mr X'.

Instead, the default position sees me indulging in a 21st-century version of the jib-top man's dance of death by selecting one of two unattractive options. I can step on the sheet forward of the car to get the load off before wrestling the securing pin

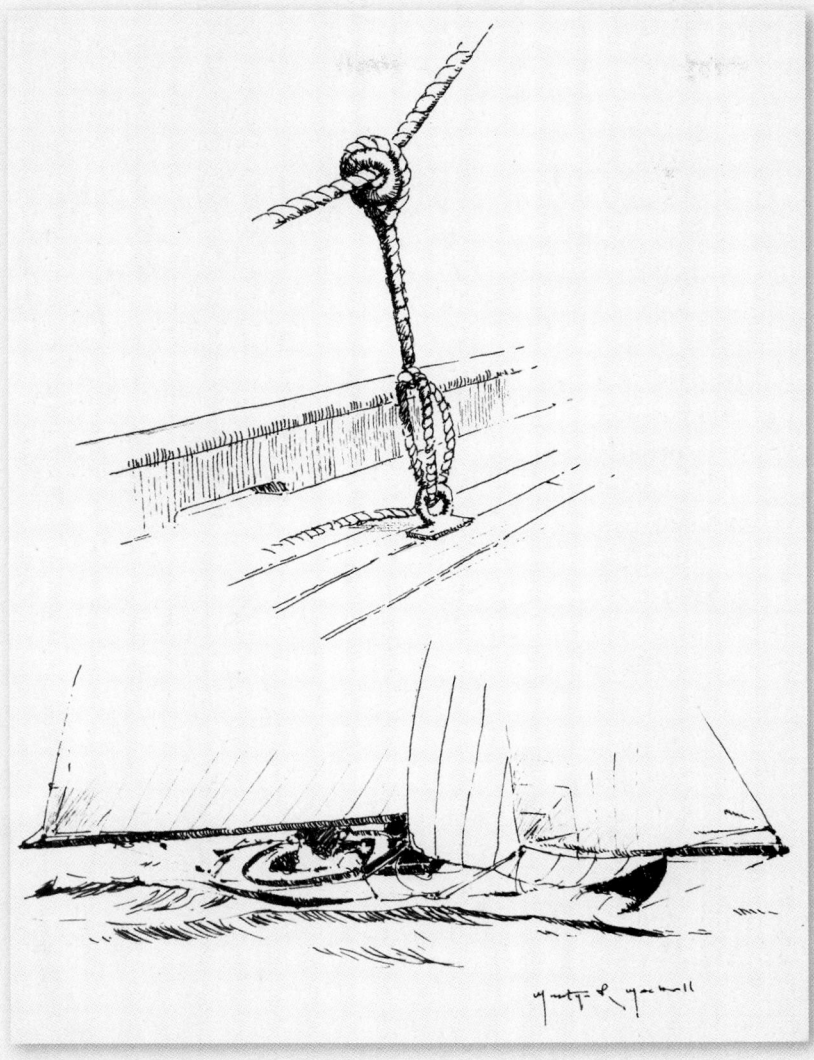

LEFT: The humble lizard is the most useful piece of gear. Lizards are even used extensively under a different name on modern racing yachts

free and trying to shunt the block forward against the upward pull of the sheet. If this fails to appeal, I might choose to let fly the sheet and take my chance with the homicidal whipping of the slack as I shove the car along the track. The soft option is to adjust the car on the weather side then tack onto it, but on a long board that's not great either. The answer is – I'll bet you've already guessed – a lizard.

I have two lovely modern composite bullseyes spliced into Dyneema® tails permanently rigged on the sheets. The tails are led aft to spare cockpit winches via turning blocks shackled to stoutly mounted stanchion bases. The result is a perfect set every time. So much more seamanlike than hanging on to the lee rail up to your knees in roaring water while ripping out what's left of your fingernails on those blasted pins.

MAST HOOPS

Last night, I poured myself a finger or two of Shackleton's whisky, recreated by the original distillers from a case found under the sheds of the great man's 1907 Antarctic expedition. A classic spirit if ever there was one. I tossed a log into the stove and, as it blazed up, I treated myself to a trip down Memory Lane courtesy of a cardboard box stuffed with photographs of my old boats. Forty years' worth were gaff cutters. Looking at the early ones, I cringed at how the sails were set up, thinking, 'If I'd known then what I know now, how that boat would have flown…'. It was only when I commissioned the newly built 20-ton *Westerman* that I came close to getting things as right as I knew how. Take mast hoops, for example. I'd recognised for decades that by far the best means of securing the mainsail luff to the spar is hoops, but life had dealt me a series of lacings and funds were perpetually short, so de-rigging the stick to slide on a set of the finest wasn't an option.

The only real downside to hoops is that, even if stitched round with rawhide, they can still chafe the mast's varnish. A liberal slushing with tallow helps and, since you will be tallowing the gaff jaws anyway, why not do the hoops as well? To offset this minor annoyance, the benefits are stacked up high. Here are just a few:

DOING THE JOB

The primary function of mast hoops, a lacing, or even – perish the thought – parrel-ball lanyards, is to maintain control of the sail when luff tension is off. This means it stays close up to the mast while it's being reefed, hoisted or lowered. Hoops do this job far better than lacings, even if they are rove to the formula promoted by Conor O'Brien. The lacing is either too tight or it slackens off when the sail comes down so that it ends up sagging away and is messy to handle.

A sail without hoops is totally reliant on throat halyard tension to hold the luff straight. This cranks up the loads on the ropes, blocks and the sail itself. Hoops help to keep the luff more or less in order, easing things off all round.

TRICING TO IMPROVE THE VIEW

Inspect paintings of 19th-century gaffers working in tight water and you will often see the tack of the mainsail triced up a foot or three. I used to follow this example when sailing up my home river at Beaulieu. The difference it makes is surprising and it is achieved with the greatest of ease. The tack of the sail is secured to the boom by a tack line, or downhaul, which passes through a dumb sheave immediately abaft the gooseneck and cleats off further aft. On large rigs, it may end in a tackle under the boom, from which it can be quickly detached for tricing up. The tricing line itself is rigged from the tack up to the gaff jaws. Here, it is rove through a single turning block, thence back to the deck. To trice up, you've only to let go the tack, heave on the tricing line and away she goes. Without hoops, if it works at all, it is so untidy as to be unusable.

A RAPID REEF

Of course, when push comes to shove, there's never any substitute for a proper reef, snugged down and tied well in. This takes time and, in many cases, a certain amount of searoom too. If you're an ambitious sort of sailor like me, there will be occasions when you are caught out and need to shorten down in a hurry. Maybe a squall has more spite in it than you expected, or perhaps you're only a mile or two from the chosen haven when the wind starts rising like the lift in a skyscraper.

This is when mast hoops really repay the investment. Heave up on the weather topping lift (if you've only one and it's to leeward, hard luck. You should have rigged a pair…), let go the tack line and trice the foot up as far as you can. The aft part of the sail doesn't change shape at all. It goes on driving with the air flowing sweetly off the leech, but the forward bottom quarter disappears. The effect on the boat is amazing. She stays in balance, but that frenetic, over-canvassed feeling is gone. You've just put in the equivalent of a couple of reefs in as little time as it takes to say 'Trice her up, Mister' to your ever-ready mate.

WIND AGAINST TIDE MOORINGS AND SCANDALISING

Nothing succeeds like hoops when you're obliged to deal with a mooring where the wind is blowing against the stream. Whether picking it up or getting under way, you can't set your main. When the boat is stemming the current, the sail will be full of wind and you won't be able to stop. In a modern yacht, there's no problem arriving at such a berth. Drop the main out in the offing, approach under genoa, spilling wind as required to stem the tide. Easy. Most gaffers don't have enough area in the staysail for this, so some main is essential until the last minute. Set up that weather topping lift and trice up hard to take off way. When you're nearly there, and still trucking on, slack away the peak halyards too. As the peak settles, the scandalised sail virtually disappears, leaving only a scruffy roll between boom end and throat.

To drop this awkward mooring, hoist the throat and trice the luff, but don't peak up. Now slip the buoy and heave away on the peak. When you're good and ready, ease the tack down, harden the luff, and off you jolly well go.

REEFING THE MAIN

Reefing the mainsail at sea ought to be routine for any sailor. The essential technique is the same whether you're on a 2020 state-of-the-art yacht or an 1895 fishing smack.

Leaving out luggers, roller reefing booms and, heaven help us, in-mast systems, the order of service goes like this:

- Set up a topping lift.
- Ease the luff down with the halyard and secure the tack reef cringle.
- Harden the halyard again.
- Bring the corresponding clew cringle down to the boom and secure it.
- Tie in the reef points.
- Let the sail take the weight and off you go.

ABOVE: A gaff mainsail can often be lowered under the weight of its gaff, even off the wind, so long as the peak is kept higher than the throat. Mast hoops help to control it once the tension is off. They also offer possibilities for rapid sail reduction

Dead simple, but for many classics there's a catch. I've never sailed a boat where bringing the tack down was a problem. On a Bermudan sail, you've only to ease the halyard and grab the cringle. With most gaffers, the first reef can be tied in without any adjustment to the peak halyard, so all that's needed is to slack away on the throat. If the geometry of your sail demands ease on the peak too, then so be it; most will be asking for this when reef two comes along.

Once the tack is secured, the fun begins. The amount of grunt required to carry the leech cringle down to the boom seems to vary with the square of displacement. On boats under 20 feet, the reef pennant can often be pulled in without any mechanical assistance. At the other end of the scale, I've sailed on schooners where the main is so colossal that it has to be dropped to the deck to shorten sail. Without a large crew who do not fear death this is clearly unsatisfactory. Fortunately, some sort of power applied to the pennant does the trick for most boats, but with a long boom there's more to it than that.

REEF COMBS

I've no idea how reef combs came by their name but, whatever their etymological origins, a good one is the key to taming the monster of shortening a boomed sail. The comb, of course, is the structure at the outboard end of the boom which leads the clew pennants down to the correct place on the spar and turns them so they can hook up to the winch, the tackle, or Mr Muscle, whichever is hauling down the clew cringle.

A modern yacht with classic slab reefing invariably sails with the reefed main entirely supported at the clew by the pennant. One end of this is dead-ended somehow on the boom and the line is rove through the clew cringle to deliver a rough 2:1 purchase. It then leads back down to a turning block on the boom and thence to a winch. With a hollow alloy boom, the block is invariably in a sheave box at the boom end, which means that to achieve the vital combination of downhauling and outhauling, the dead end must be sited exactly right. Ideally, this is via a running bowline around the boom and under the loose foot of the sail. Countless boats of all sizes have sailed round the world with these arrangements.

Traditionally, things were very different. The clew was hove down either by a permanently rigged reefing tackle under the boom or by a roving tackle dragged from its locker. Either way, when the mate was satisfied that the clew was snugly down on the spar, some likely lad was sent out onto the boom to pass an earring, the name given to a lashing holding the reefed clew in place. The tackle was then slacked away and the points tied in. I've sailed on some big classics where this sort of thing still goes on. Lashing the clew down made some sense in a world where rope could be unreliable. In our liberated times of polyester and Dyneema® cordage, it is superfluous on any but the most enormous yacht. I have crossed oceans 'on the pennant' in substantial craft and it is easier and safer, so long as nothing is going to let go. The secret is a proper reefing comb.

In theory, a classic reef comb – Bermudan or gaff – is two lengths of hardwood, ideally oak, attached on either side of the boom. At each reef, one side will have a hole for the dead end of the pennant, the other side carries a sheave through which it can run. Holes and sheaves are often alternated for reasons I have never understood. In real life, you don't know which tack you will be on when reefing time arrives. Why not have a sheave on both sides so you can tie a quick figure of eight to leeward and heave down from the uphill deck rather than knee-deep in green water in the lee scuppers? A stopper knot works just as well in the swallow of a

RIGHT: Reef lacings offer an alternative to points for securing the bunt of a reefed sail. They are favoured by long-boomed yachts as the lacing will even out the pull, which may not happen with points. Here, the hands line up to pass a reef lacing preparatory to pulling down a reef while the helm tries to steer high of the course to keep the weight out of the sail

block as it does in a straight hole.

The comb should be sited so the pennant, when hove down snug, makes an angle of around 45 degrees at the boom. This secures the clew 'down and out' as it should be.

That's the basics. Now for the practicalities:

Sailing on the pennant, the rope and whatever it is attached to or runs through is taking all the weight. With a heavy boom, a mainsail full of wind and the boat falling into holes in the sea, the loads are prodigious. A stout polyester pennant isn't going to let go, so the comb must be above suspicion. The obvious answer is to run the sheave pins clean through the boom as bolts, carry them on to the outside of the comb, and rivet them off. This is fine if you don't mind hammering bolts through spars, although many consider this to be asking for long-term rot as water seeps in. A refinement we worked up for one of my boats was to make up bronze straps that ran under the boom and inside the comb with holes at either end for the bolts to pass through. The straps took the weight, the pins could be shorter and the whole thing was bomb-proof. It looked good too with the strapping disappearing under the comb. Both ends of the most appropriate strap reappeared above the comb to carry lugs for the topping lifts. Very neat, and nothing to go wrong.

A final refinement I inherited on an early gaffer answered the question of what to do with the dangling pennants not in use. Obviously, these are best left rove up so as to eliminate any nastiness when reefing time arrives. I think the arrangement probably originated with Chris Waddington at Wicor Marine, a man who always runs a tight ship. Rather than ending a foot inboard of the deep-reef sheave, the comb was carried forward with small knobs worked into it onto which the spliced ends of the pennants were hooked until required. As well as being tidy, they were available without poor sailors having to stretch out and grab hold of them in an awkward sea. The whole effect was of a piece of sculpture much admired and totally successful. I saw some terrible weather with that boom. It always looked yacht-like and it never budged a millimetre.

HARBOUR-STOWING THE STAYSAIL

Nobody wants the hassle of unhanking the staysail and sending it below every night during a cruise. Jibs might have to come off, but staysails are better stowed on deck. The soft answer is to leave it hanked to the forestay and stuff it in the bag. If the bag is colour co-ordinated this isn't a bad solution, but it's a lot more elegant to make an art form of stowing it.

The Thames sailing barge gives us the lead. The foresail – the barge's equivalent of a cutter's staysail – is bent to hanks seized to the forestay, so removing it is not a serious option. Instead, it is tightly rolled, secured with a long gasket spiralling around it, then hoisted well up the forestay after releasing the tack. It's thoroughly seamanlike, it gets a hefty parcel of cloth out of the way of the lads cranking the windlass and it keeps the sail away from any mud coming aboard, but it would look eccentric on a yacht or a working cutter. The concept of rolling the sail away and hoisting it holds good, but a

LEFT: A tight harbour stow on a staysail can be a happier solution in mid-cruise than stuffing a wet sail bag down below

different technique is called for here.

Lay out the sail, still hanked on. Heave the clew aft and do what you can to roll or flake the sail into the extended 'bag' formed along the foot. The process will present no issues until you approach the tack. There's no neat way of rolling this in, so the trick is not to try. Instead, unshackle the tack and wrap it around the rest of the luff before re-shackling it. You may have to release the bottom hank, or maybe not, but once it's done, you'll find the bag along the foot works a lot better too. All that remains is to find a soft length of three-strand to lash up the roll nice and tightly. I favour marline hitches myself, but however you do it, hook the staysail halyard to the clew and hoist away, leaving a sweet curve in the stow. Stabilise the result with the sheets and Robert's your uncle.

TILLER LINES

The other day I was sailing on a gaffer of some substance when I noticed the crew complaining of tired arms and stiff shoulders. She was tiller steered, as any boat under 50 feet ought to be, and when my turn at the helm came around I soon had sympathy with the grumbles. In calm water, the pressure of the weather helm was considerable. When we passed into the rough stuff, the kick was enough to pull my arm out of its socket.

Yet tillers were standard equipment on all but the smallest craft in the days before wheel steering took the sting out of things. Eighty-five-ton sailing trawlers were tiller steered; ditto pilot cutters at 30 tons or so; even Thames barges in the early days had no wheel, and *Dawn* still sails the Essex seas under the command of her noble tiller. Boats vary, of course. Some hefty beasts are so well balanced that you'll often see them with a hand directly on the helm. The mighty *Jolie Brise* is a case in point. More often, however, they are like my 40-foot *Westernman*. Fast though she was, she would exhaust even the strongest muscle-man in half an hour, juggle the rig as we might, but if a tiller line were used, the problem disappeared.

Tiller lines cover a wide spectrum. On smart yachts they may be spliced-up permanent fixtures with leathered blocks, belaying pins and all the paraphernalia of a proper job. My own boats have never risen to such heights. On *Westernman*, for example, we just lifted the mainsheet coil off its belaying pin and passed a bight around the end of the iron tiller which terminated in a ball to stop the line slipping off. The helmsman perched comfortably on the weather cockpit coaming and held the return part of the sheet. The line rendered freely around the tiller, yet enough friction was generated to take the spite out of the operation. Reeving it round the tiller and back created a whip purchase which immediately divided the load in two. The friction did the rest. When the breeze piped up some more, we'd take a round turn on the tiller. This carried all the load. It was slightly more cumbersome than the half-turn of the straight whip, but in practice it didn't matter a jot.

On long legs, we'd dead-end a short length of pensioned-off 14 mm braidline on the tiller, lead it through a quarter block then back round the tiller for a bit of extra purchase. It was lovely to handle, and when it finally chafed through after some hard use we tossed it in the bin and cut off a new one. Cheap at the price, the hands reckoned.

Tiller-line steering relies on a steady supply of weather helm which most healthy sailing craft are more than happy to deliver. Rather than heaving and grunting, the helmsman waits for his moment then, when the boat takes a lurch and the weight comes off the helm momentarily, he grabs a swift ten degrees of weather helm and claps on the extra turn. Once she settles down, the boat will slowly begin to bear away. The turn is

RIGHT: Tiller steering is far more sensitive and faster than using a wheel gear. So long as it's backed up with a proper set of tiller lines, it doesn't have to be tiring on a well-balanced boat

now eased until equilibrium is reached. A well-balanced craft will then trundle along as straight as a gun barrel for a minute or three, often with the tiller line secured and the helmsman taking things easy. In due course, the helm will either need easing a little more, or the person steering waits for the boat to give him his chance then helps himself to a few degrees when they are offered. It works like a charm and a skilled operator can stay in control for hours without his arms dropping off.

A boat that does not carry appreciable weather helm will need a dedicated tiller-line system with blocks on either side to enable the stick to be pulled either way, but in smaller craft, and some larger ones too, this is rarely necessary.

STANCHIONS AND GUARDRAILS

In our safety-conscious times, these are something of a controversial subject for the owner of a classic sailing yacht or workboat. Back in the golden days before World War II, few boats carried them that were engaged in cruising, fishing, piloting or inshore racing. Surely nobody would argue with the plain fact that they looked all the better for it. Working craft of any stature usually had – and still have – bulwarks which confer more than a sense of security, while yachts almost invariably feature a toe-rail against which a foot can confidently be braced when necessary. That being said, despite these age-old solutions to the issue of keeping the crew the right side of 'the wall', things have moved on and many people do not feel comfortable without the stainless steel ring of refuge served up to the modern yachtsman as a matter of course.

Leaving aside some of the good solutions and horror shows that have arisen to deal with this on traditional craft, it's worth taking a critical look at what's on offer to 'Boat-show Man' as he stumps up large sums for a CE-marked bundle of safety features. When I brought my own yacht into the UK from her native United States, I was obliged to spend a shocking amount of money convincing the EU inspectors that she was seaworthy. I understand that, in spite of Brexit, little has changed on this front. The boat is as classic an item as any GRP yacht can ever be. One issue flagged up was that her double guardrails were too high for the specification defined on the inspectors' clipboards. This brought me up with a round turn and I queried the logic.

'Aha,' they said wisely, 'people might fall under them.'

The idea is, of course, ridiculous. By comparison, plenty of today's guardrails I've sailed with are far too low, pitched perfectly to catch poor sailors at knee height and flip them neatly over the side in short order. The stanchions are sexily angled outwards, presumably to create the illusion of deck space, leaving the guardrails more a hindrance than a help to anyone unlucky enough to have to negotiate the lee side deck in a seaway. Those contemplating rigging

RIGHT: Guardrails are no substitute for a good set of bulwarks, although the best of all solutions can sometimes be to augment one with the other

guardrails to a classic need to bear all this in mind, but are guardrails really what we want? After all, they get in the way of sheets, they don't generally do much for the look of a boat and sailors managed without them for generations. There weren't all that many hands lost overboard, were there? Or perhaps there were. Statistics were either not kept or have been cryptically hidden from the likes of us, so we have to rely on anecdote and impression.

Speaking as a chap who for 40 years loved his classic vessels, raced them, showed them off and sailed them on the deep seas, here's my take on the subject:

If I'm crossing an ocean, or just sailing offshore in conditions likely to knock up a sea, guardrails are almost a must. They might not save you from falling overboard if you're thrown by a heavy lurch and are not clipped on, but you can use them to steady yourself while moving around, which means you are far less likely to be thrown off balance in the first place. For me, what might be called the 'gold standard' for a passage with guardrails would be an overnight trip across the English Channel. But what about the rest of the time when I'm racing round the cans with the staysail sheet snagging and the mate in trouble for leading the jib topsail the wrong side of the wretched wires?

The answer is easily removable stanchions. Forget pulpits and pushpits. They are invariably an eyesore and serve no purpose in traditional craft. Pulpits were developed to supply a solid support for people changing headsails at sea on racing yachts with the bow plunging under. What could be less appropriate on a gaff cutter,

yet such monstrosities are still out there. If you happen to have inherited one, give the boat a break and throw it in the skip now. Stanchions should be a sensible height and be shipped or removed readily. With bulwarks it's easy. The metalwork drops in through bushed holes in the capping immediately forward or aft of the through-deck stanchions. The base can then either sit in a socket solidly fastened to the face of the wooden stanchion or slot into something similar on the deck beneath the hole. Either way, the metal stanchion is securely held. A split pin or some such can stop it lifting out. As to the guardrails themselves, the days of stainless wire, tiny bottle screws, swaged ends and goodness knows what else are gone, together with all the associated expense. Welcome to the brave new world of Dyneema® core.

Forget the fancy sheath beloved of chandlers that hurts your eyes and is inappropriate in the extreme. Instead, choose the basic core version, perhaps in tasteful grey. It's stronger than wire, less than half the weight and the great thing about it is that you can do the whole job yourself with only a simple braidline splicing fid for a tool. Youtube is awash with videos showing how to splice this amazing product. I recommend the Mobius Brummel eye splice. It's dead easy and it's also bulletproof. Attach the standing end to the appropriate stanchion by cow-hitching the eye of the splice. Work a thimble into the other end to take a lanyard. Buy some suitable fittings for the lanyard – I've used small 'whisker-shroud' plates fastened to the bulwark capping, sited so that the guardrail angles down and ends sweetly somewhere near the bow and the stern. Set them up nice and tight with the lanyards and that's it – instant guardrails.

When you arrive, it takes only minutes to whip out the stanchions, coil up the Dyneema® and stow it all below where it belongs for most of its life.

STOWING SAILS

A sail cover can hide a multitude of sins, with the front runner a poorly stowed main. On a modern yacht with a stack pack and lazy jacks, a tidy stow is nigh-on impossible, so zipping up the bag when the shorelines go on is the decent thing to do. For the classic sailor, gaff or Bermudan, the neatly rolled, crease-free alternative is a thing of beauty. There should be no rush to cover it therefore, unless it's to be left soaking up UV from the sun for a day or squadrons of incontinent herring gulls are lining up for a bombing run.

I learned how to stow a mainsail on an American schooner in the days when 'Dacron' cloth (known as Terylene in the UK) was in its infancy. Back then, what we now know as polyester canvas didn't come stuffed with today's fillers. It is these that make new sails the stiff and slippery nightmare to fold away that we all now suffer. These sails do set beautifully, so maybe the price is worth paying, and even on the stowage front there's hope for the future. As the filler degrades, or falls out, or whatever else happens to it with time, the fabric becomes more pliable. It grows ever more friendly with passing years until, at its last hour, it is as kind as the cotton or flax that our grandparents could stow to perfection – as long as it was bone dry.

If a sail is still crackly with filler, the only way to stow it is to flake it onto the boom. This is best achieved by lowering it slowly while the bosun heaves the leech out hard, keeping the foot flat while flaking it down. Any spare crew will assist along the bunt, clapping ties on as necessary to keep the whole slippery horror from sliding onto the deck. There is no pleasure in this job on a windy day, especially if there is a sea running, and however hard we try it's never going to approach the beauty of an old-fashioned harbour stow.

Gaff is easier to flake than Bermudan, because the leech is more vertical and the final stow is tied up to the gaff with no chance of sliding off the boom. The sail is lowered on both halyards, keeping the gaff more or less at its sailing angle until the throat hits the gooseneck. The peak is then lowered steadily while the flakes keep piling up.

When the sail is more pliable, either because it is of natural fibre or through the passage of time, the misery of flaking becomes history. A neat, tight stow is now readily achievable. Different boats have different methods, but here's one that works on small sails, and is fine at least as far up as 1,000 square feet. If the boom's normal resting height makes reaching it a stretch, lower it with the topping lifts until you can reach the sail easily, taking up slack on the sheet. Gaffers will have to ease the peak halyards as well to keep the gaff handy to the boom. Once the sail is stowed, you can top the boom back up.

This time, the sail is not stowed while it's being lowered; it is dropped smartly onto one side of the boom. The ship's rugby player

now grabs the leech. Starting at the peak of the gaff, or the head if the sail is triangular, he or she works down to the clew, hauling aft all the way, assisted by more of the crew if necessary. This removes any bunch-ups of canvas. The leech is now hauled hard aft from a point two or three feet above the clew depending on the size of the sail, forming a sort of bag between the fold created and the boom. The person on the leech now works towards the head or the peak, hauling aft all the time while bundling the sail into the 'bag'. The rest of the team follow suit along the bunt, or body of the sail. When it's all in, the crew shake the bag together to tighten the contents before working it up onto the boom in a neat, crease-free roll.

If the sail is loose-footed you may have to miss out the shaking phase to prevent the stow from tumbling out under the foot. The ties should be ready rove between the foot of the sail and the boom so there's no scrabbling for them while trying to hold the beast in place. The whole job can be done single-handed on a 30-footer. As sails get bigger, the more hands the merrier.

On a gaffer, ties are led over the gaff and under the foot of the sail, but never around the boom. Leading ties between the gaff and the head of the sail is a bad idea. Not only does it look awful, it stretches the head-rope into bights.

LEFT: Stowing sails is very much an art. Here, the sail is being flaked as it is dropped. When it is down, the foot will be rolled around the flakes to create a neat stow

When the stow is complete, the boom is topped up to a perfect angle and gaffers can set the peak to suit personal taste. I like to see it parallel, or slightly up at the throat. Scandinavians keep their peaks well up, but in all cases, that tight roll sheds any rain. Water affected the lifespan of sails cut from natural fibre, which is prone to rot with damp. The sailors of old prevented this with a proper stow and, as is so often true, what working people developed for pragmatic reasons still pleases the eye today.

SAIL TIES

When is a sail tie a gasket? I have to make that clear before describing what I've found works best for securing canvas. The term gasket is little used today in yachts, probably because a gasket is a permanently rigged sail tie. For the most part, we no longer use these. Gaskets are found spaced out along the yards of square riggers, all ready to go for the hands as they lay aloft to tidy up after the sail has been furled from the deck with buntlines and clewlines. They are too long to be conveniently carried in a seaman's pocket, so they stay up there, hanked neatly with gasket coil hitches awaiting their moment of glory.

A schooner I once sailed on board carried gaskets secured through varnished wooden rails running along either side of the bowsprit. The rails took the form of 1½-inch (38 mm) square strips screwed on halfway between the horizontal and the vertical. Together with the spar itself, they supplied a useful platform for flaking the sail when stowing and a relatively secure foothold for young seamen walking out to the cranse iron. Once the sail was folded, it was secured by taking one gasket from each side and tying them over the sail in a reef knot. On the square rigger, the gasket coil is released so the long gasket hangs down forward of the partly furled sail. It is then passed around the canvas three or four times and tied off.

A sail tie is quite different because it usually arrives at the job either draped around the sailor's neck or stuffed into a pocket. On a bigger boat, the mainsail ties will be too bulky for this treatment and are generally deployed over the boom before the sail is dropped so there's no scrabbling around for a tie while hanging onto a heavy bunt of folded sailcloth.

For most applications, a tie should have an eye either spliced or sewn into one end. The plain end can be passed through this after wrapping the sail, allowing an instant 2:1 purchase for racking the stow up tight. Securing is also simplified by simply passing a bight around the back and through the standing part to form a slippery hitch. Easy to tie, even easier to let go.

So, what's the best material for a good sail tie? I recently sailed aboard a Norfolk Broads gaffer from Hunter's Yard at Ludham, and a thoroughly seamanlike little craft she was. Lovely, soft three-strand sail ties were in profusion, small enough to pocket, strong enough to do the job 'and some'. On larger boats, you can't beat stout, firmly woven webbing. I had a set on my 35-ton pilot cutter. Each was four or five feet long, measuring 2½ inches (63.5 mm) across the flat with big eyes sewn into the ends. Rope would have scored the varnish. These were kind to spar, sails and cold, wet hands. Perfect.

FLAKING FOR THE DROP

Assuming that a long-coiled halyard will run cleanly when you take it off the pin is expecting a lot. To be absolutely sure it behaves itself as it snakes cleanly upwards, the best plan is to flake it before letting go. Unlike a coil, a flake starts from the bitter end. This is because the end will be at the bottom when the action commences and the rope will run from the belay, not the end. You can't coil like this, of course. A coil must begin from where it's made fast. If you try forcing it from the loose end, the natural turns built into the lay of the rope compound towards the immovable part at the pin and the coil is untidy and potentially dangerous.

With a flake, so long as the rope is allowed to follow a natural figure-eight pattern, it doesn't twist up at all. If there isn't time for such finesse, work through the rope towards the pin, encouraging it to fall as it will. Just remember that either way you must arrange for the bitter end to lie well clear. Leave it under the heap and it can get sucked into the running line and bring a smooth job to a messy halt.

One final thought. A while back, I wrote

about flaking ropes and was finger-wagged by an ancient mariner insisting that the correct term was 'faking'. Suit yourself, is what I say. So long as the halyard runs free, what's in a name?

STOPPING THE RATTLE

Modern yachts lead most of their halyards inside their hollow metal or carbon masts. Very tidy it is too, and good for minimising windage. Since this is often impractical with timber spars, we of the classic persuasion carry ours outside. There's much to be said for this in terms of accessibility, but it does render the ropes liable to slap against the mast in harbour when the wind gets up. The noise is unacceptable, especially when it means the varnish is being steadily eroded beyond the reach of easy patching. Out in the open at anchor it's a particular annoyance and many's the day I've tottered on tiptoe trying to frap the bights out to the shrouds as high as I can reach. Any frapping job is most effective when the business is done halfway between fixed points, but I never could achieve this ideal until I met a man on the East Coast who had solved the problem. The trick doesn't generally work for gaffers because of the siting of the spreaders, but it's ideal for a Bermudan spar. Here's what you do:

Make up a neat wooden thumb cleat and secure it well outboard on the forward or aft face of the spreader, open end away from the mast. Now ease a bit of slack into the offending halyard, grab it at shoulder height and flip it out a few times until the thumb cleat hooks the bight. Harden it up again and you won't hear a peep out of it until you whip it free before weighing anchor. If you've two halyards causing annoyance, have one cleat each side and enjoy perfect symmetry.

CHAPTER FOUR
NAVIGATION

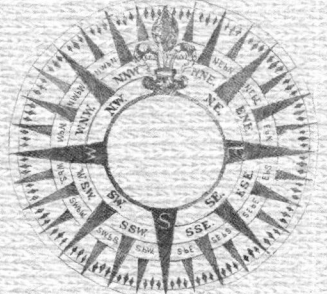

While boat building has crept onward slowly and steadily to incorporate modern materials such as epoxy and adhesive mastics, navigation has undergone a total revolution since the arrival on the scene of GPS. The 1990s saw almost-perfect fixing available regardless of visibility without special equipment beyond a simple, affordable receiver. Twenty years later, the chart plotter became a viable instrument. It is now standard equipment on most leisure craft of any substance and the mindset of the navigator has been changed for ever. Lost in history are Captain Lecky's 'L's of navigation – 'Latitude, Lead, Log, Lookout and trust in the Lord'.

What follows in this brief section is a reminder about the continuing importance of the steering compass, the barometer and, most important of all in these electronic days, the 'paper' logbook. Without the last item, the mariner is truly lost should those fine buzzing instruments ever go absent without leave.

Lastly, come one or two time-honoured methods of managing without any instruments at all, ancient or modern. The Vikings, crossed and recrossed the Atlantic without compass or chart. Many among their number doubted whether the world was round, and while the idea of relative north–south distance had been established, numerically defined longitude lay centuries in the future. If all else fails, then we must learn, like them, to note the run of the sea, the movements of birds, the nightly position of the stars and, if we want to go west, to follow the setting sun.

BOX THE COMPASS

'Steer northeast by east a half east.'

What's that in new money, you might well ask. Perhaps you'll also be wondering what it's doing in a book about what's in the Bosun's Bag, so I'll tell you. This work is a collaboration between me and my artist pal Martyn Mackrill. Every so often, we meet for a pint and swap ideas. One evening in the 'Jolly Sailor' Martyn showed up with a lovely drawing of a traditional 32-point compass with not a numbered degree to be seen. For a moment I questioned the relevance for a page that's supposed to be carrying advice and tips from a sailor, but then I thought again. If you've an old boat, it may be that her original steering compass is like the illustration above. You could, of course, replace it, but it's far better to use it.

Long ago I was a gash hand on a small sailing ship whose compass card had points,

not numbers. Neither the skipper nor the mate was handy when it came to encoding courses and bearings from the chart into old-fashioned compass subdivisions. The chart was black and white with depths in fathoms, but its compass data read out in degrees, either true or magnetic, depending on which of the concentric roses you selected. For reasons I still cannot recall, I knew about compass points. Having sat through an early 1950s education I also had a pretty sharp grip on basic mental arithmetic, so I was appointed navigator's mate with the task of translating from the chart to our beautiful compass as it rode and tilted in its binnacle.

Every child learns the four cardinal points and every sailor who uses the Shipping Forecast hears 'northeast', 'southwest' and the rest on a daily basis. Halfway between 'northeast' and 'north', with impeccable logic, lies 'north-northeast' and so on. Now it starts to get interesting. Lying in the gap between 'north-northeast' and 'north' is 'north by east'. The interval between this and due north measures 11¼°, which might seem an obscure number until you find that by multiplying it by four, you get 045°, which is the numerical equivalent of 'northeast'. 'East' is 090°, and so on.

So now we know why the Colregs define an overtaking vessel as more than 22½° abaft the beam. What they are trying to say is *'two points* abaft the beam', which is a lot easier to understand once you have a handle on what a point is. There are 32 of them in the circle of 360°.

Steering on a compass like this is a lot less taxing than peering at tiny numbers. 'South by east', for example, has a clear mark on the card's rim and all the helm has to do is hold this around the lubberline. Many would argue that trying to steer a sailing boat to anything closer than ten degrees is fantasy and there's some sense in that. However, one can do better. Suppose the magnetic course laid off on the chart, duly corrected for deviation, reads 276°. 'West' is 270°. 'West by north' is 281¼°. If we want to hit the spot more or less, we can steer 'west-a-half north', which is halfway between the two. It's as easy to keep the lubberline midway between a couple of points as it is to hold it on one, so that'll do for the course. Should the course be 273°, for example, 'west-a-quarter north' cuts the subdivisions down to less than 3°, which is as good as you're likely to get out of a human helmsman. Once again, it's not as difficult to visualise a quarter point as you might think. The eye backed up by its brain in the absence of a processor can 'do' quarters surprisingly well.

In a world where navigators rely more and more on electronic numeric bearings and autopilots to steer their ships, equipping with a compass that features real points is as practical as it is traditionally correct.

A CLASSIC LOGBOOK

Decent logbooks seem to have gone out of fashion. I've been on several yachts lately that either don't have one or, worse in some ways, use those store-bought fantasy volumes with columns for stuff I've never heard of and nothing for what I need. How dare the publishers presume to tell us what to log? Who do they think they are? We all should decide what we want to know, over and beyond the navigational basics.

Despite the rise of electronic navigation, the primary purpose of the logbook remains what it has always been: to supply the data required to produce an accurate estimated position at short notice. In ancient times, of course, this was standard practice and responsible pilots did it either every hour, or when they deemed it necessary. Today, the information serves more as a backup in case the plotter goes AWOL, but the principle is the same. The starting point is still a 'last known position', plus the course steered and distance run between then and now. How we log this is up to us, but if we don't bother and the screen goes blank out of sight of land, we're as lost as we ever were.

My logbooks date from the 1970s. I've kept them all, not so much for the star-sight altitudes duly recorded 'according to the Act', barometer readings, weather, engine hours and so on, but because my crew write in them at length on passage, then use them as visitors' books when we arrive. You can't do that with a tailor-made job. These are hard-backed exercise volumes. One side of each spread carries the columns I want. The other side is for comments, rude or otherwise, with space for creative guests. Here lie classy artwork, children's pictures, poems of quality and limericks so scurrilous they are beyond printing. Photos are stuck in alongside menus, beer mats, bus tickets and even a 'Get out of jail free' card, just in case. You never know what you'll discover.

Fill the book in as you go along and note anything that should be entered into the 'jobs to do' list that should be inside the back cover. If you don't write down that the mousing has disappeared off the bobstay shackle when you first see it, you'll forget about it and the next thing you know the spar will be pointing at the sky with the jib

RIGHT: Filling in the logbook on the hour at sea supplies a rhythm for the watchkeeping, records the ship's position so it can be referred to if necessary, and supplies a history to enjoy in years to come

luff looking out for better weather.

Another vital element of the logbook is more pages at the back filled with notes regarding the running of the ship. Things you analyse once, then forget so you have to do it all over again next time. I keep any observations about compass errors here, so I have a running deviation card always to hand. Rigging notes save ages spent messing about looking for a good lead. 'Peak halyard fall runs inside topping lift on port side. Standing end runs down to purchase – outside to starboard.' 'Staysail sheets lead outside cap shrouds, then inside aft lower.' 'Slings for lifting boat are to be sited at second stanchion from the bow and ditto at stern.' It all adds up to a private bosun's manual, and it costs nothing but the discipline to enter details as they occur to you, an ordinary book and a cheap biro pinched from the harbourmaster.

Go on, start running a proper logbook. In years to come it may serve you in times when laughs are hard to find.

TAP THE GLASS

Life for the sailor is incomplete without a barometer. I've one at home which my father tapped every morning as he went to work. Seven decades on I still listen to its quiet, metallic response as the needle pops up or down and I reset the datum marker. On board the boat, a less venerable instrument has its readings recorded more formally. At sea we log it on the hour for a heads-up on the real world to augment the virtual

ABOVE: Tapping the glass and logging its reading is a vital part of any ship's record-keeping

arrows on the computer screen. If there's no barometer column in the book, tapping it is a waste of time.

In the trade winds, the needle should be dead steady inside a two-millibar rise and fall – high at 1000, low at 1600. Once you've established the pattern, if the reading moves more than a couple of points beyond it, watch out! Things may be more erratic in higher latitudes, but when the eastern sky flushes red before sunrise and the glass has dropped five points overnight, never mind the internet. Go to sea if you must, but stand by your reefing tackle.

THINKING OUTSIDE THE BOX

Sailors must always be ready to improvise. Finding himself at sea with no egg cups, the sailor of my ancient anecdote scratched his head, then produced a spare toilet roll. It supported his three-minute soft-boiled perfectly.

A similar attitude saved a World War II submarine navigator I knew well, who was stuck in the skipper's head compartment, which was also his position for action stations. Having forgotten his parallel rulers and dividers, he used instead the ever-handy toilet roll as a sliding parallel ruler off the compass rose on his chart. For distance, he laid the skipper's toothbrush along the latitude scale, measuring off the miles with his thumbnail.

BACK TO BASICS

When all your electronics have gone phut and you have unwisely left your Walker log gathering dust in the loft, don't despair. 'Course steered and distance run' makes the basics of dead reckoning. We can take a decent compass for granted. Even the most modern yachts have yet to abandon this vital component. The question is how to determine distance run. Here's what to do:

Find a length of small stuff, the lighter the better. Go to the toolbox and extract the tape measure which all well-found vessels carry. Tie one end of the string to an old piece of wood and measure off 84½ feet (25.8 m). Toss the wood over the side, noting the time to the second. Let the line run out. When it fetches up short, note how many seconds elapsed and recover it for next time. Now divide the number of seconds into 50 and that, believe it or not, is the speed in knots. If it takes 8 seconds, you're logging 6¼ knots. It may not be perfect, but it beats an electronic paddle wheel that's a few degrees off line or has chummed up with a strolling mollusc.

CHAPTER FIVE
MISCELLANEOUS

Every bosun's locker carries a container, a tub, or even a bag, full of bits and pieces that can't be categorised in an organised shelving system. My own, for example, features a large wooden box I've had for 40 years and more, labelled 'miscellaneous small fittings'. When I'm in need of some obscure piece of chandlery with the nearest dockside store 1,000 miles away, a delve into its depths often supplies an item that can be made to work. By any standards, the contents are a shocking jumble of rubbish, but, on the day, they can turn out to be solid gold.

Among the top-class bronze left-overs from some long-forgotten job undertaken decades earlier, are bits of old pump and obscure strips of metal found lying in the dust under a boatyard workbench, picked up because 'they might be useful one day'. An old motorcycle inner tube will have managed to tangle itself with a coil of copper tubing thrown away by a prodigal plumber and fished out of a high-street dumpster, and so on. Rubbish, yet in the hands of a creative ship's husband these odds and ends might save the boat and the lives of all aboard.

When it comes to organising the contents of a book like this, there's many a subject that just won't fit. Hence this section. Making an oil lamp work as it should is an art in danger of being forgotten. Judging from what one sees in movies and on the TV, it already has been, so we deal with it here and our lamps glow with warm light through crystal clear glass chimneys. How did our forefathers deal with chronic weather helm? What is the best way to mill the stock for table fiddles to make life at sea civilised instead of a camping trip in a fairground crazy house? Why would I remove a perfectly serviceable boom from my staysail, and what are the pros and cons of a fixed main boom gallows? How do we keep awake in the depths of the middle watch at 0230, and what on earth use can we make of sacks of sawdust culled from the local boat builder's back door?

These subjects, and more, are the topical equivalent of the 'miscellaneous' box in my bosun's locker. Somewhere in the following pages, there is something for every one of us.

ABOVE: A perfect dinghy sitting apparently weightless on calm water. This painting has no relevance to the text opposite but it was too beautiful to leave out!

FIDDLES

Whatever your vessel, the fiddle rails in the accommodation probably came as part of the package. If she's a one-off, they may work fine, but decades of disappointment with production craft have led me to the conclusion that some of the well-meaning folk who fit them out have never been to sea. Tiny fiddles that can only be described as 'nominal' rely largely on that magic non-slip material sold in chandleries to take up some of the slack in moderate conditions. This fabric is a tremendous innovation and far superior to the traditional wet tea towel, but if you're building a boat from scratch or enjoying the benefits of a major accommodation refit, fiddles are one area where your efforts can shine.

Two main variables define a fiddle. Shape and height. There's no universal rule about height, but shape should be cast in stone, or at least sawn from a nice piece of teak. If you look at most 'store-bought' fiddles you'll see that the inner face that does the work has been chamfered to create an attractive appearance, while the outer face is vertical. This is the reverse of common sense. Trying to locate a plate or a mug against a bevelled fiddle rarely works and if anything slides up against it, the angle provides a perfect launching ramp to propel it into free flight. A vertical inside face offers a solid support for a proper parallel-sided mug, and steadies the lip of a plate without compromise.

Now, what about height?

The ideal height for a fiddle varies with the job it has to do. Chart table fiddles exist to restrain charts, books and, these days, a laptop computer. These are not prime suspects for low-level take-offs, so while rolling and heeling are a bigger menace than pitching, an inch or maybe 1½ inches (25–38 mm) on a fore-and-aft face is generally sufficient if, like me, you sit looking 'abeam' at your chart table. You're going to be stuck with an uncomfortable fiddle to lean across, but it can't be helped. A chart table where the navigator faces forward or aft is easier. The fiddles to counteract heeling can then be as high as you like, while the one in your lap may realistically be smaller, or even non-existent.

One often-forgotten factor in chart table design is to avoid curved fiddle corners. They cause chart corners to crumple and rise up so that the dividers slide across the paperwork, dodge the fiddle altogether, take a dive off the desk and impale the cook. Keep it square, and leave the corners open so you can sweep off the bits of india rubber left after a serious plotting session, even if the aesthetics take a small hit.

Laptops on chart tables present an opportunity for the creative owner in the form of removable fiddles. You won't want the computer deployed all the time, so any permanent fiddles somewhere in the middle are going to be a nuisance. You'll need the flat, uninterrupted surface to lay out a chart or for pouring cocktails after a tough passage. The beauty of movable fiddles is that they can be retro-fitted by anyone who can drill a hole in a straight line and has access to a hacksaw.

Fiddles dedicated for the laptop can be fairly low because it won't be sliding around trying to leap off, and if they're too high they get in the way. You'll have a sheet of the magic non-slip cloth to stabilise the PC in case it's a shade small for the enclosed

The Saloon

ABOVE: A lovely traditional small-yacht saloon. There's no place like it on a windy night in good shelter. Note the useful fiddles on the table and shelving. They make all the difference

area. The fiddles are made on the bench as individual items. Don't try to match them up with bevelled corners to form an open-topped box. They are secured on the table top by carefully driving a bronze screw into the bottom surface of the fiddle, then sawing off the head to leave a 3/8-inch (9.5 mm) peg. The female side of the arrangement comes from holes drilled into the top of the chart table to match the screws and bushed with yellow metal inserts epoxied in. This can be achieved with tiny copper tubes or something similar. Match the screws to the tube, not vice-versa, because screws are readily available in various sizes. Tubing may not be.

Movable fiddles can also be used on the saloon table, and now comes the time to pass on where I learned about this useful arrangement. My pilot cutter *Hirta* carried her riveted iron water tank at the forward end of the saloon sole. It had been there since 1911 when Pilot Morrice of Barry and the foreman of Slade's yard in Polruan decided that this was the best place for the weight. They were right about that and, as a spin-off, the tank gave them an ideal site for a saloon table. I know not whether the lovely table I inherited was original, but it fitted the tank perfectly and had flaps all round for the convenience of the diners.

The table top itself had fixed fiddles on all four sides, an inch or so high. The flaps were protected at their outer edges by removable fiddles along the lines described above. This meant that if you were on the windward side, your bacon and eggs rested against the outer face of the fixed fiddle, so there was no need to use your removable one. The chaps on the lee side set theirs up and it prevented their plates from dropping into their laps. If we were putting on a fancy dinner in harbour, we dispensed with all the movable fiddles and enjoyed a table as clear as the one back at the homestead, except for the inner fixed fiddles which reminded us that we were in a fine old sailing vessel. What could be simpler, or more effective?

For reasons that must surely be obvious, fiddles in the galley should be high and robust, but, like all fiddles, they must comply with the final rule: every surface protected by fiddles will have to be cleaned, decrumbed and generally maintained. If the fiddle fence is not broken somewhere, this will be a wretched business. The answer is to break the fence neatly at the corners so that even the most casual of dishcloths can sweep the remains of the toast into a waiting hand.

RIGHT: It's too easy to rig up an electric riding light nowadays, but the whole ritual of hoisting an oil lamp at anchor is part of the breathing of the ship's life. With a good dioptric lens, it can be seen from afar

OIL LAMPS

They're at it again. Every time I settle in to enjoy a period film or TV drama, all credibility is expunged by what really is the simplest of errors. Western movies are a good example. Here comes The Man with No Name to shoot the forces of darkness back to Hell where they belong. I'm hooked into the story up to my neck until I notice a sooty lamp chimney that reveals beyond doubt that the director understands nothing. And when the villain tosses the lamp onto the handy pile of straw to incinerate his victims in their humble cabin, you can be sure the glass is as black as his hat. I'll bet the chimneys were just as awful in the BBC's dear old *The Onedin Line* all those years ago, but the ancient skipper Mr Baines could have told them a different story. Anyone who looked that much like Captain Birdseye would have known from boyhood the way to treat an oil lamp.

How, I want to know, do these people imagine their characters operated indoors after dark by the light of oil lamps rendered useless by blackened glass chimneys? Of course they didn't. It isn't a lifetime ago that I'd a home in the Yorkshire Dales where some of the outlying farms still relied on Aladdin lamps. In my own world, I've had three boats where the main lighting below decks was paraffin-fired and I still use an oil riding light with a noble dioptric lens. Nobody in their right mind, either afloat or up in the hills, would tolerate blackened chimneys for a moment. Firstly, you're paying good money for the paraffin and if the glass is opaque you might as well pour it down the sink; and secondly, because getting a crystal-clear glass is dead easy.

CABIN LIGHTS

Here's the secret, step by step. Some riding lights vary in detail, but I'll deal with them further down the page.

- *The right fuel* – no need for expensive 'lamp oil'. I've never used it. British or US paraffin/kerosene from any roadside garage or old-fashioned hardware store is fine. I did once suffer a foul batch in the Canary Islands which blackened everything, including my deckhead, but that was a one-off, it was far from home and has never been repeated.

- *Clean the glass well* – very carefully, with warm soapy water and a soft cloth, wash it out. You may need a wooden spoon to ease the cloth down inside the glass where the non-metallic handle will guard against damage. The bosun's toothbrush is useful too. Dry the glass and do not let it near a flame until all moisture has quit the scene. Get the rest of the process right and you'll only do this once a week.

- *Trim the wick* – wind it up so it pokes out above the burner and cut it square across with sharp scissors to remove all carbon. This is a monthly job, or less.

- *Lighting up* – having filled the reservoir to a half-inch (12.7 mm) from the top, wind up the wick so it's clear of the burner. This encourages it to light. Put a match to it, then turn it down as low as you can without extinguishing it. As the flame takes hold it will rise a little.

- *Glass on* – at this point, install the still-cold glass chimney into its holder. Give it a moment to absorb a little heat from the tiny flame, then wind up the burner until the flame is level with the slot.

- *Slowly does it* – you're nearly there now. Tentatively feel the chimney to see how it's warming up. When it's getting hot to touch it'll be safe to wind the flame higher, knowing you won't crack the glass. Now it's just a matter of experiment to see how far up you can set the wick without the flame actually licking the glass and without any suggestion of black smoke. Keep an eye on things for a few more minutes to make sure there's no hint of smoking, and that's it. Lovely warm light just as it should be – and always was in the days when no alternative offered itself.

ANCHOR LIGHT

A decent riding light consists of a cylindrical can, or cage, with a glass strip to disseminate the light from a lamp burning inside. Its structure allows air to circulate to the lamp and it has a sophisticated draught-excluding system to keep the flame from being blown out. The lamp itself usually comes in one of two forms. The first is the same in principle as a cabin light. The second has the guts of a cabin light, but no chimney. That is supplied by the body of the lamp. Whichever version you have, the lamp must first be lit and settled before it is offered up to the cage. A cabin-lamp type is lit exactly as described above, but note that when it is inside the cage with the doors shut, the cage too will heat up and draw the flame upwards, so set the wick on the low side before inserting it.

A 'chimneyless' lamp is lit and simply inserted into the cage in a draught-free environment – often the saloon. As usual, be aware that as the cage heats up, the flame is going to rise. Experience, and trial and error, will show how much wick to give it, but once the flame's in place behind that dioptric lens, what looked like a modest glim will shine out like a beacon.

My videos on lamps are at: https://youtu.be/gfX67kcCx5M and https://youtu.be/Y8lBws-WEPU

LEFT: Keep the wick trimmed and the chimney clean, and you'll be surprised at the quality of light from a good cabin oil lamp

Christmas Eve without electricity

I doubt there's a decent classic work boat or yacht left without at least a nominal oil lamp in the saloon. If there's a full complement, her crew are well on their way to Christmas on board without using any power at all. What a fine aspiration that is!

We've sorted the illumination on the previous page. Now, what about beating the cold? Remember we're not using any electricity, so blown-air systems are dealt out. And a good thing too. Nasty, noisy things. Drip-feed diesel is OK, but it's hard to beat a solid fuel stove for atmosphere and lovely, thick heat. Fire was one of the first things that set us apart from the beasts of the field. A man needs to build one every so often to keep his humours balanced. Lighting my cabin stove is a delight every time, unless I'm close-hauled on the starboard tack when it is guaranteed to blow back and fill the saloon with smoke until the chimney hits critical temperature.

If you have a problem with smoky start-ups, sticking your blow torch up the chimney before lighting is a popular answer among experienced firemen. The hot flue sucks the smoke away as soon as you approach the stove with a match. If you aren't on a power-blackout Christmas, the wife's hair dryer will produce an equally pleasing result.

I keep my anthracite nuts in crisp zip-up bags bought from an old-fashioned hardware store for a pound a throw. They only last a year or so, but they are effective. They mean zero mess except for a bit of ash dust for the hand-brush at clean-out time, and if you keep the kettle on top, you've hot water on tap as well.

As for the cooker to roast the turkey, it's a while since I was skipper of the 1913 55-ton cutter *Jolie Brise* in the far-off days when she still enjoyed a coal-fired galley stove. The range kept the ship warm and dry, but it did carry downsides, including a long wait for a cup of tea if the cook forgot to riddle it, and getting shot of the daily galvanised bucketful of ashes. Most of us now cook on safe, clean gas, so there's no amps squandered there. The traditional paraffin stove can also do the business, but most examples struggle to accommodate the bird.

So there we have it. Christmas Eve without power. Silence at 0100 as we sit in awe, hearing only the faint rustle of the wicks burning and a soft clink as a coal falls in the grate, waiting for the flooding tide of Christmas morning, and God with us.

LEFT: With the stove burning brightly and the lamps glowing on the bulkheads, a Christmas cake on the table and a bottle of the right stuff to wash it down, all that's needed is a chosen shipmate and there is no better place to be under Heaven

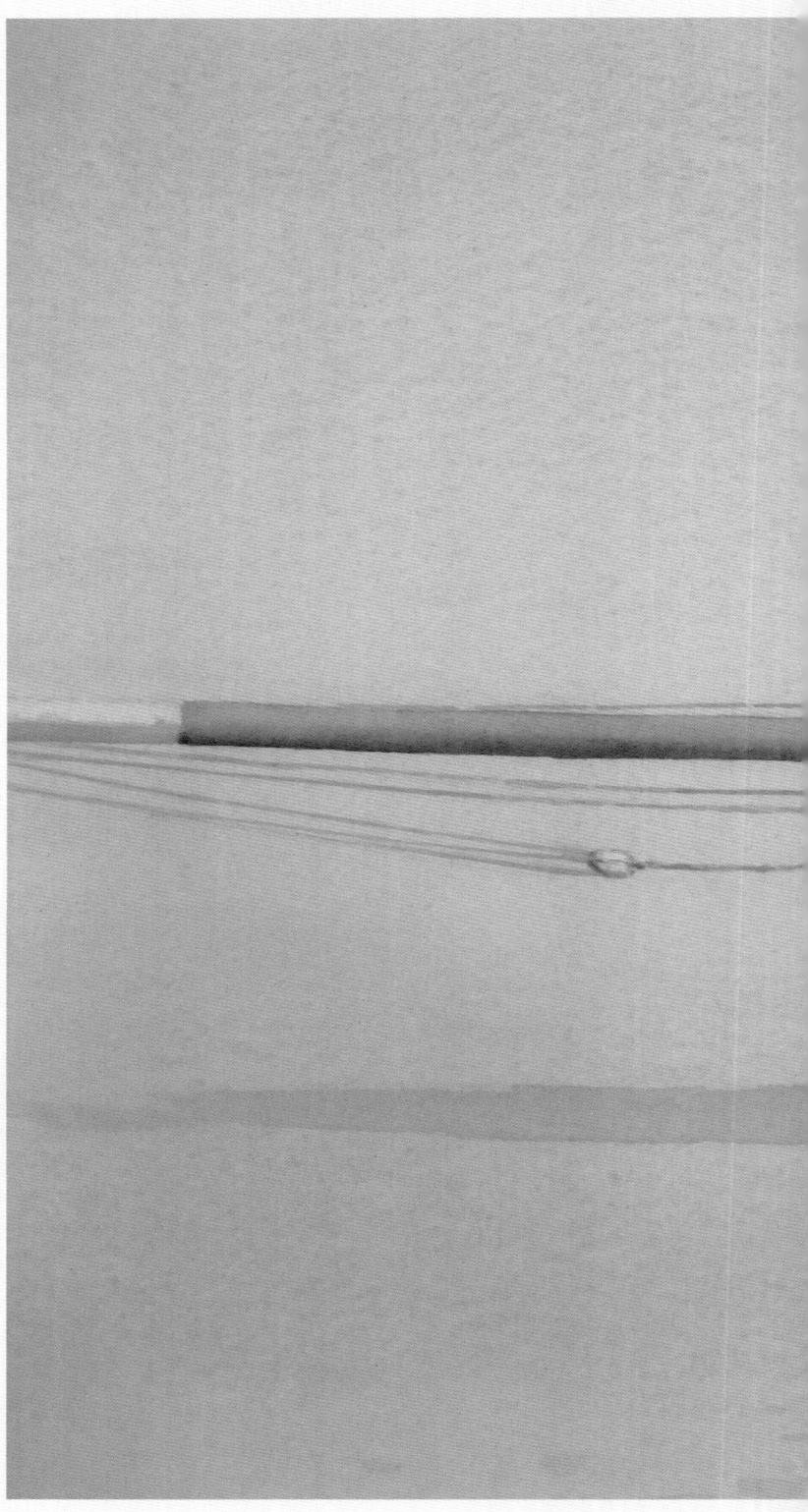

RIGHT: Keeping the bobstay clear of moorings or the anchor cable by tricing it up out of the way is an age-old technique that has largely been forgotten. This smack has classic external chainplates sitting outboard of the bulwarks

Chain plates — internal and external

INTERNAL CHAIN PLATES

If your chain plates run inboard of the planking, perhaps down through the deck, there's little to be done with them beyond making sure they don't leak. A chain plate weeping through the deck does more than rot the planking, it can worry away at its own structural integrity until one dark night it gives up the ghost and lets go. Even stainless steel is not immune to this insidious weakening so, as soon as there's a hint of a 'bubble and squeak', we must find it and stop it in its tracks. There are all sorts of ways of filling the gap around a through-deck chain plate, but success usually lies in the compound. I made a discovery about this a few seasons back that I wish I'd found years ago. When the contents of one of my saloon lockers began to take on the nature of a well-used bath sponge I followed the standard discovery procedure, starting with the wet bit at the bottom, then onward and upward until the cap-shroud chain plate 'fessed up. Sealing it was easy. The gap had never been caulked with cotton or oakum. It relied entirely on mastic.

The procedure is simple. Back off the shroud tension, lift the covering plate if there is one, and gouge out the old sealant from the trough around the chain plate itself. All clean and dry? Now, here's the thing: don't even think of opting for one of those compounds (no names, no pack drill) that works as an adhesive as well as a sealant. Using them is a loathsome procedure. Go instead for a butyl product which skins over, never goes off completely and is dead easy to clean up. Gun it in and screw down any covering plate to 'squidge out'. If there isn't one, just smooth it off and that's the problem solved for another season or two. At least when it starts to leak again, as it surely will one distant day, you can remove the old mastic easily rather than face the misery of trying to gouge out adhesive sealant.

EXTERNAL CHAIN PLATES

There's a great deal more to classic chain plates than meets the eye. External chain plates must be long enough to spread their load, but not so long as to appear ridiculous. They are secured with bolts passing through holes drilled into the topsides and some sort of meaty woodwork inside, ideally a frame. So long as the bolts are a snug, gently driven fit through plenty of timber and the plates are well bedded, leaking should never be an issue. The main area of concern is the aesthetics.

When deciding how a boat should be presented, it's always a sound plan to start with a trawl through photographs of original examples of her type. It'll be ten to one that 'back in the day' the chain plates were painted over, not picked out. Those guys knew what they were about and I can think of at least three good reasons why they did this:

One, the continuous paint film helps keep the water out from behind the plate. Two, it makes painting the topsides a whole lot easier. Three, and by far the most important, picking out the chain plates halfway along the boat breaks up the sweet flow of her sheer, the sweep of her planking and everything else you can think of.

Also offensive to the educated eye is the practice of accentuating metal fittings on the planking at bow and stern. These might be bracing pieces for backstays, chafing plates for the anchor chain, forestay reinforcement or any number of other items. Like the chain plates, they all should disappear behind the topside enamel as they did until the relatively recent fashion for showing them off.

Where there is a wale strake below the sheer, the chain plates should be forged to wrap around it. To inset the plates into the wale is to compromise the extra strength the fat plank is meant to confer and it looks terrible.

Chain plates should not be made of flat bar. The inner surface is plane to lie snugly against the planking and take the bedding mastic, but the outer is gently curved for appearance and to prevent it catching on passing docksides or other boats.

When it comes to the bolts themselves, let's have no more hexagon heads. A chain-plate bolt should have a round coach-bolt head that nestles against the plate. The square inside the head locates in a square socket all ready for it in the chain plate. That's how it always was done. It pleases the eye, snags nothing, and it's correct.

Weather helm and movable ballast

Once upon a time, as fairytales usually begin, I sailed in a boat that had truly shocking helm balance. This, however, was no fairy story; it was horribly real. She was a well-built little 28-foot sloop from a classy designer, but when I joined her to assist the owner on his inaugural passage she was not at all happy. The weather helm was such that when she took a gust as we left harbour she almost tacked herself.

One gets used to this sort of wretched behaviour in certain modern yachts with flat floors, excess beam aft and no forefoot, but this boat's sweet lines bore no relation to such monstrosities. Her rig seemed all in order too. There was no retro-fit over-hanging boom or shortened bowsprit to play havoc with the designer's intentions, but I did notice one thing. As I joined her, she looked perhaps a little down by the head. Perhaps, I wondered, she'd been trimmed like that on purpose to allow for a couple of hefty crew in the cockpit. This is sometimes a good plan with smaller boats, but there was a pair of us back aft right now and her manners were still shocking. What was going on?

An hour or so into the trip I went forward to use the head. As I sat in mute contemplation of the nicely varnished mast, the comparative silence was broken only by what I took to be the slosh of the bow wave on the planking. I've heard a lot of water running past planking in my time and this didn't sound quite right. It was more like liquid sloshing around in a tank and it was coming from somewhere up near the stem. I completed my private mission, then squeezed myself into the small fo'c'sle to investigate.

There, on proud display, was a large stainless water tank making gurglings as if it were as full as it was ever likely to be. I estimated it to be around 50 gallons, and 50 gallons is a quarter of a ton. The tank had obviously been sited so as not to rob the main accommodation of space, but it was wrecking the trim of the boat. I went back aft and reported. The owner, who had personally had the tank fitted as he liked plenty of water onboard, was reluctant to believe me, but as we laboriously pumped the tank dry, the yacht was steadily transformed into the beautifully balanced lady she should have been.

I left the boat soon afterwards, so I can't report on whether the tank was ditched to make the boat into an honest girl once more or whether the lust for a hot shower proved too great a temptation for her owner, but the incident reminded me about how critical fore and aft trim can be.

When we first launched my boat *Westernman*, a new 40-foot gaff cutter, we found we could ease her tendency to weather helm by shifting a quarter-ton of lead trimming ballast from the mast area and packing it tightly under the companionway. I had picked up the trick by reading Maurice Griffiths who claimed similar success with a smack before World War II.

I've no direct experience of ballasting issues where the boot is on the other foot, so to speak, but sometimes a boat is slow to tack where really she shouldn't be. When a backed staysail is needed to help her round,

ABOVE: One pig at a time!

or maybe if she sometimes misses stays altogether, shunting ballast forward will probably cheer her up no end.

If you have a long-keeled sailing boat that is reluctant to balance as she should, things might not be so extreme as they were with the water tank, but it's still worth taking a hard look at her trim. And if some smart individual on the dockside suggests that you're wasting your time because when you shift ballast aft you tip the rig back too and thus increase weather helm, he's talking rot. The effects of the two are hardly comparable. What looks like a done deal on paper is often set at nothing when Old Man Wave takes hold. The masthead moves feet at a time as the boat pitches gently in a seaway. The ballast stays right where you put it.

BOOM GALLOWS

One of the decisions that must be made when restoring a classic sailing craft, or commissioning a new one, is what to do about supporting the boom when it's not in use.

Four choices spring immediately to mind. The first is to follow the lead of the Bristol Channel pilots on their 50-foot cutters. These redoubtable mariners opted to have nothing to do with superfluous hardware. Instead, they were content to leave the spar hanging in its topping lifts. I followed their approach for 15 years with an original example and can report that there is a lot going for this solution. Their conclusion was that a permanent boom gallows can get in the way and that it costs money. Booms on these boats were typically around 30 feet long and of solid pitch pine, so they were heavy. Their twin topping lifts were suspended from plates through-bolted at the cheeks of the hounds immediately below the bolsters where the shrouds looped over. They pulled back against the forestay, joining the aft 'swifter' shrouds in giving the mast a degree of rake which assisted with backstaying and looked good into the bargain. It made for one job less when lowering sail, because the boom didn't have to be located into a notch on the gallows with the boat rolling in an awkward popple. At hoisting time there was no overhauling of sheets and sweating on topping lifts to raise the boom clear of the support.

There were two downsides. One, that couldn't be denied, was that the arrangement made for a lot of heavy point-loading on the rig 24 hours a day, even in harbour. The second was that when the mainsail had to be dropped at sea in extreme weather with the boat standing on her ends, there was nowhere to secure the boom. Leaving it simply hanging in the lifts was not an attractive option. As it happens, when I was confronted with this rare situation, an easy answer presented itself. The boom was original, the boat still had her 1911 cockpit and deck furniture, and, guess what? The boom end settled down on deck between the cockpit coaming and the bulwarks so sweetly it hardly needed lashing.

Just for the record, when we built *Westernman*, the 40-foot cutter that replaced the old pilot boat, we followed suit and rigged her with no boom support. We never missed it except when lying at anchor in a bit of a sea. The boom then had to be restrained in two directions. A quarter-tackle rigged temporarily worked wonders.

At the other end of the scale to offering the resting boom no support at all comes the full-fat gallows. Built with a good, solid frame of galvanised iron or bronze, this is capped by a teak rail with three notches, offering stowage amidships or to either side. The notches are dressed with rawhide so the spar's finish remains undamaged. Once in place with its sheet bowsed hard down, the boom is rock solid, putting no strain whatever on mast or gear. A further benefit is that a stout boom gallows makes a marvellous grab rail at a sensible height. It can be used for stringing up awnings and for leaning on while yarning with the chap on the next boat in a raft-up. What, you might well ask, is not to like? I had one on a different boat I sailed many thousands of miles. On the whole I was pleased with it, but it wasn't all win-win.

It would have been nice to say that we always dropped the boom into the gallows to reef as some authorities seem to recommend. We didn't. Getting it into the notch in a seaway was just too hit-and-miss, with one hand at the mast on the topping lifts and the other in the cockpit waiting for the boom to hit just the right spot, then heaving down on the sheet 'PDQ' before it slipped out again. If you failed to secure the boom, the slack topping lifts let it fall below the level of the gallows. On the next wave it smashed into the uprights. The best outcome was then crushed wood fibres and mashed varnish. At worst, the heavy spar did actual damage to the gallows. In fact, the whole business of landing it in exactly the right place in anything but flat calm was so fraught that it was a major nuisance. I suspect that the problem was made worse by the fact that most of the time, the boat had no working engine, so holding her up head to wind for more than a few seconds was far from easy. Also, the teak had to be varnished, so that was another job on the list. On balance, by the time I changed up from this boat to the pilot cutter, I could see why the pilots did as they did.

As in many things at sea, perhaps the best solution lies in compromise. The greatest pilot cutter of them all, three-times Fastnet winner *Jolie Brise*, a boat far better sorted than most, uses a full-on gallows that hinges down flat when not in use. It never gets in the way and seems somehow to disappear when not deployed. With her 38-foot boom, this gives all the benefits of a solid support in harbour and none of the disappointment at sea.

The fourth answer is the varnished timber 'scissors' brought out on deck as a fine yacht enters port. These open up into an elongated 'X' shape with the lower ends slotted into sockets sited exactly where they should be. Nothing holds this device up until the weight of the mighty boom lands on it. Then, so long as the bosun has set the angle just as it should be, gravity ensures that it can't possibly go anywhere, while the tops of the 'X' make the perfect place to hang the sweetly coiled mainsheet.

WINDVANE

Readers might wonder what on earth windvane self-steering has to do with classic boats. The answer is, quite a lot. One vane-steered yacht whose pedigree nobody would question is the late Col 'Blondie' Hasler's *Jester*. She was a folkboat, one of two in the inaugural 1960 Observer Singlehanded Transatlantic Race. Various innovative self-steering options were tried among the five entrants, including Sir Francis Chichester's 'Miranda'. This took the form of a large sail that pulled the rudder directly, but it was Hasler's pendulum-servo system that came out tops.

Those of us who sail classics short-handed face the same challenges as Chichester and Hasler, but more answers are available today. A cheap, cheerful and surprisingly effective solution for small well-balanced yachts can be a simple cockpit autopilot of the generic 'tillermate' variety. The over-riding advantage of these is that when not in service they can literally disappear below decks and nobody knows the difference. For longer-range use, experience has taught me to carry a spare. They don't last forever.

Hefty below-decks autopilots are fine – again, for well-balanced boats – but they are power-hungry and after a week or three the quiet buzzing starts to drive me nuts. That's because I'm worrying about the 75 amp hours it could well be eating every day, the complex 'brain in a box', wear on the windings of the motor and the rest of the machinery until the noise finally stops. The batteries can then breathe a sigh of relief and I'm back to the tiller. A windvane does away with all this anxiety. Blondie Hasler sailed the Atlantic in complete silence and probably only used his battery to power a simple lamp to read an improving book.

When my wife Roz and I set sail for the southern hemisphere in our 1903 Colin Archer-built gaff cutter *Saari*, it was 1975. Windvanes had been around for a few years and had been quickly accepted by the relatively small band of ocean wallopers then plying the deep seas. One or two other successful forms had arisen, but I kitted *Saari* out with a second-hand pendulum-servo gear based on Hasler's original, made by a man named Max Gunning. I don't suppose Gunning had a factory. For all I know, he knocked them up in his garage, but it was a strong, galvanised, agricultural sort of job. If anything should fail, it could be fixed by the user or some pliable local blacksmith. In my case there was no need. It worked from 'Day One', and it kept on working through thousands and thousands of miles, in rough weather and calm, storms and light zephyrs. Once it was fitted, we never steered again. Remember, this was a 12-ton gaffer which is not always the most delicate craft on the helm.

The pendulum-servo gear uses water flow to beef up raw wind power. The windvane is adjusted so as to feather when the boat is on course. When she wanders, the vane receives wind on one side or the other. It reacts by pivoting. This activates the servo paddle which is a deep blade cutting through the water below it. The paddle is hinged fore and aft, so that as it is twisted off the 'feathering' position by the vane, it is kicked up sideways like a pendulum by the water flowing past it.

If you doubt the power, try it with an oar as you buzz along in the dinghy. This swinging movement to one side is transferred to the helm by lines joining the paddle to the tiller or to a drum on the wheel. As the paddle is displaced, it drags the helm with it. This steers the boat until she is once again sailing at the original angle to the apparent wind. Vane, and hence paddle, now return to the 'feather' position and the process ceases until repeated again. The net result is a surprisingly straight course in most conditions and I would advise anyone unused to it to avoid being trapped between the tiller and a cockpit bench with the gear in full cry. I have suffered nasty bruising and on one wild night I almost ended up with a squeaky voice.

There are two unavoidable downsides for a gear like this: it doesn't enhance the

ABOVE: My Colin Archer-designed cutter, built in his yard in 1903, steered herself thousands of ocean miles entirely by means of a pendulum-servo windvane

appearance of the stern and mean-minded harbourmasters may bang you for an extra pound or two for the added overall length. As to ongoing maintenance, my Gunning used turning blocks. The pins did wear out from the constant working, but I'd sourced my blocks from a boat jumble and new ones would probably have fared better. The tiller lines also chafed a bit, but they were cheap enough. A dab of oil here and there, and that was maintenance done with.

The vanes themselves are 'fit and forget' items on a modern yacht with her short boom, but on *Saari* or, I expect, your boat, with a respectable overhanging boom, what then? In my case, the vane stuck up higher than the boom end and was well inside it, so I had to whip it off each time I tacked. A bit of a nuisance, that's all. If I forgot, it snapped off, so I just sawed up a new one from a sheet of ply that I carried under the main bunk. Ply has a hundred uses in emergencies. This is just one of them. Regarding the closeness to the boom end, I never fathomed what was going on with the apparent wind across the vane when I was close-hauled, but I knew that if I set it more or less fore and aft, the boat would settle down at around 45–50 degrees from the true wind.

One final word about windvanes on classics. I've already noted that they don't do a lot for the appearance of the boat, but most can be dismounted and sent below in an hour or two for regattas. If yours cannot, wear it as a badge of honour. How many of those concourse yachts have just sailed in from Greenland?

KEEP AWAKE

Watchkeeping in the days of merchant sailing ships was straightforward. Four-hour sessions were the order of things, starting at midnight with the wretched 'middle watch' until 0400. As the on-deck crowd tumbled below for what was left of the night, the sleepers turned out, and so it continued at four-hour intervals until teatime when the 1600–2000 session was broken by the dogwatch system. The division of this watch into two 'dogs' served to shuffle the watch order so that nobody had to stand the middle watch on successive nights.

With a four-person crew, plus skipper and cook, this system still works as well as any. I've used it on ocean passages and noted that, within their four-hour stint, the watches generally make their own arrangements so that, with two nominally on deck, one is relaxing somewhere – perhaps even in the bunk – while the other is alert. So far as I'm concerned, they can sort out who does what and when among themselves. There's no need for complicated rotas.

Four hours might seem a long stretch, but given a bit of responsible cat-napping, it soon goes by. Apart from the ever-cheering sight of dawn crawling over the weather rail, the best of the day is at 1800 when the turn of the dogwatch brings all hands on deck for a yarn and a modest crack at the skipper's rum.

Many of us now make our voyages two-up. After a few false starts, my wife and I have settled for the simplest system of all. Watches start after dinner – usually at 1900 ship's time. We take three-hour stints until 0700 brings us both out for breakfast.

The autopilot or the windvane does all the work, so we can relax, read, make a snack, contemplate our mortality or do whatever suits us, as long as we keep a good lookout. Wherever possible, tweaking the peak or heaving down a reef is saved for the change of watch. During the daylight period, we rest according to needs and conscience.

With a third crew member, the night-time gallops by with 'two hours on, four off'. Luxury!

USING UP OLD SAWDUST

Last week, I happened to be at Hunter's Yard on the Norfolk Broads as the boys were working the traditional greasy ways to launch off their fleet of classic charter boats. The yachts are 70–80 years old and, after a winter refitting inside a dry shed, many are going to leak for a while. Some do, some don't, but the chaps are ready. As soon as a boat is secure alongside, whether she's leaking or not, they dig into a large bucket of sawdust and tip it into the river around her. Then they sink it with a dinghy paddle and encourage it to drift under the keel. As the seams weep, the ingress draws the sawdust in with it and it helps the boat take up more rapidly. The sawdust is so soft that it does no harm at all as the seam tightens.

In case you are thinking this sounds like an old wives' tale, I've seen fishermen doing the same thing with sacks of the stuff in Ramsgate harbour and in the Caribbean too. There's usually plenty kicking around in boatyards. As long as you're not sinking so fast that only the fire brigade will do, why not give it a try?

MASTHEADS AKIMBO

A ketch, a yawl or, perish the thought, a classic schooner, with masts sagging outwards at the top is a grim sight indeed, yet every day two-masters suffer this indignity. Unless a specific reason existed to do otherwise, traditional sail plans went to some pains to keep two or more masts parallel when viewed beam-on. If a boat is designed with the masts spreading like the twin fingers of derision, the only thing to do is sell her now to someone who knows no better. Usually, though, it's a matter of how the spars are set up and can soon be put to rights.

There are, of course, honourable exceptions. Some working ketches set their mizzens with a degree of forward rake to achieve cantilever support for a mast that cannot have a standing forestay because of the main boom. If you're building a replica of a Swansea or Virginia Capes pilot schooner, you can forget the rule too. These unique and effective rigs with their steeply raked mainmasts and vertical foremasts reflected the European shallops which preceded them. They baffled logic in the 19th century. They still do now.

RIGHT: Running off before a storm is sometimes the best survival option. A single headsail, far forward of the pivot point of the boat, makes steering as easy as it is likely to get in seas like these. It's a grand thing to see the two masts of this Fife yawl parallel to one another as they should be

CHAPTER SIX
MAINTENANCE

When I was a young sailor sitting under my boat in an old-fashioned yard, disconsolate at the amount of work I still had in front of me before I could go to sea, an elderly man called out from the next-door yacht, 'Don't let it get you down, Son. The more you put in, the more you'll get out.' Time has proved him right. Some of the jobs that must be tackled to keep a traditional vessel in seagoing condition can seem endless, even insurmountable, but all must be faced just the same. Caulking a flush-decked 50-footer singlehanded against a ticking clock is a daunting proposition, but dealing successfully with such a task brings a depth of satisfaction unknowable to the average owner of a production yacht.

Happily, it's not all grit and bleeding hands. Everybody finds their own little Nirvana in the maritime workplace. For some, it might be laying on the final coat of topside enamel, others may delight in lining up a hefty propeller shaft to a delicacy measured in thousands of an inch. As for me, I've always looked forward to working on traditional rigging. I enjoy setting up shrouds with dead-eyes and lanyards. I love judging the tension in the wires from my own experience rather than a store-bought strain gauge, while the smell of the Stockholm tar oozing out of a tight serving under my well-worn mallet on a spring morning is an annual delight.

This section isn't a textbook on yacht maintenance. Many specialists are more qualified than I to write one of those. Rather, it's a series of reflections drawn from a life spent learning how to do it myself. The trick is to find a place where others are working on their boats, and happy is the unofficial apprentice with a benevolent yard foreman watching over him. Friendships spring up among people with shared interests. Solutions to problems are offered, some bad, some priceless, but all must be weighed up in light of what is realistic at the time and within the budget.

Long ago, I stood back from a job to admire my handiwork. It wasn't perfect, but I reckoned it would get me to sea. I said out loud, 'That's good enough.'

A man walking by turned to me and announced,' "Good enough" is not good enough. There's only one standard, and that's perfect.'

All very well, but that poor soul never did finish his boat. When I returned with 10,000 miles under my keel he was still there, and he still hadn't launched off. The

RIGHT: The bosun's chair really concentrates the mind. You want to have everything you need at the first hoist, because nobody wants to pull you up a second time

truth is, we all must find our own standard. If it falls short, the final judge and jury is the sea which, while sometimes good to gamblers, takes no prisoners when battle is drawn. What's the standard, then? Will it hold up under the prolonged attention of waves and wind? So long as it passes this test, whether or not you make it look beautiful is up to you, but it doesn't do to forget that when it comes to boats, what *looks* right generally *is* right.

SLUSHING DOWN AND OTHER UNCTIONS

Aboard a working square rigger, the subordinate officers such as bosun, sailmaker and cook traditionally enjoyed certain 'perks'. Some of these were recognised by the management, others not, but one which was universal was the cook's right to harvest and sell 'slush', the main by-product of his culinary arts. When salt beef or pork was boiled up, large quantities of fat floated to the top. The 'doctor' scooped this off and stored it away. One use was to 'slush down' the steel wire rigging. The stuff wasn't ideal, but it was available. An arrangement was reached with the mate and away went the crew with rags, buckets of slush and bosun's chairs.

I've had a lifetime of galvanised wire and I still have a tub in my shed labelled 'slush'. Mine isn't old pork fat though. Over the years I've tried most things for my standing rigging and the best mix I've come up with is, roughly, 30% Stockholm tar, 50% boiled linseed oil (must be boiled), and a good dollop of real turpentine. The turps helps it mix and aids penetration. Even if it didn't work, it would be worth using just for the smell. A traditional boat that doesn't whiff of Stockholm tar is only giving her owners half the satisfaction they deserve.

The boiled oil helps the mixture skin off in due time and the tar blackens it nicely. After a few seasons of liberal application, the residue fills the lay of the wire, making it virtually impervious to water. The wire, unless it's been spliced instead of turned and seized, will then last indefinitely, and the cost is modest. The only downside is that my recipe may take a few days to go off properly, so don't ask Aunt Jemima to tea in her best skirt for a week or so.

These and the following products were once available from any store that styled itself a chandlery. Those days are long gone, but a sensible Google search will guide readers to a supply. Some unlikely high-street options still exist.

- Stockholm Tar – available from horse copers or via the internet. Prices vary, so buy wisely;
- Boiled linseed oil – available from the internet or all good hardware stores;
- Real gum turpentine – no 'substitute' please. Ditto.

TALLOW

While cruising Tierra del Fuego, that thrifty mariner Captain Joshua Slocum came across a barrel or two of tallow that nobody seemed to have charge over. Always with a weather eye for profit, he took it aboard. No doubt he sold it in due course, but I expect he kept some for himself, because he knew well that no gaff or lug-rigged classic boat should go to sea without a supply of tallow. My own stash lives in a well-built yellow plastic container originally labelled 'ghee', gleaned from the bin behind a Southampton Indian restaurant. I apply it with bare hands to the leather on gaff jaws, mast hoops, gammon irons (for bowsprit retrieval) and anything else that needs cleanish, cheap lubrication that won't wash off with the first wave. There's no need to scrub your hands afterwards, either. Just rub it in. It's a totally organic product that can do you nothing but good.

I'm never quite certain what tallow is, but it has something to do with butchers' shops and animal fat. Beef is preferred. If you run out of lard or get fed up with healthy olive oil, you can also fry with it as did Captain Slocum. Very tasty it is too.

- Tallow is available from the internet or various electrical suppliers who sell it to assist in running cables.

SEIZED BOLTS? NOT ON MY BOAT

Nothing beats tallow for gaff jaws and running bowsprits, so there's always a screw-top tub in my bosun's bag. Tallow falls short, however, when it comes to easing and protecting threads on bolts and machine screws. It's a sad fact that a spannered-up galvanised shackle will seize when loaded, doused in sea water and left to its own devices. Even high aloft out of harm's way they still weld themselves shut, and don't even talk about the mayhem that results when trying to undo any that have lived under water on a mooring riser. The answer to this is not to buy expensive grease from the 'swindlery', it's to acquire, for the price of a pint in a London pub, a jar of lanolin. Dip the threaded shackle pin or the bolt end into it before assembly and carry on as normal. As soon as you start winding the screw you'll feel the difference. It snugs home a treat, and once you've graunched it tight with the big shifter it'll never let go until you want it to. Even five years on, it'll come undone without a struggle.

I acquired my potful 40 years ago from a lifeboat man who used it to slush down cross-Bristol Channel swimmers and there's plenty left. I note that the elixir is now best purchased on the internet under the guise of a beauty product. You get a lovely container with a flower on it. Despite this nonsense, it works on a rusty thread the same as always, and it's good for your hands too.

KISS THE GREEN GOODBYE

Every vessel that is laid up out in the weather ends up with nasty green growth on her fine teak or pine decks; any covers kept in place over the winter suffer the same fate. Time was when I used to spend long periods scrubbing away at this without conspicuous success. Indeed, as we all know, over-scrubbing of laid decks is a sure-fire formula for major expense in a few years time when we've pummelled the pith out of the timber and the bungs start poking their heads up. I'm delighted to announce that all this misery is a thing of the past.

Browsing the pages of the owner's manual for a new Hallberg-Rassy yacht, I discovered that these Swedish gurus of quality tell their customers not to scrub their decks, but to treat them at the beginning and end of the season with a product called 'Boracol'. Originally marketed as a fungicide, this clear liquid penetrates the wood and does away with any algae fancying their chances of setting up home. It then hangs around for months, doing the deck no harm at all, but ensuring the menace doesn't return. Application is dead easy. Pour some into a bucket on a dry day, cable-clip a 4-inch (102 mm) paint brush to a broom handle so there's no need to bend down, and literally paint it on. Next, toddle off home, returning in three days to find your decks totally free of green. Give them a good rinse off with a hose, and that's the way they'll stay all season. A miracle product if ever there was one. And wait till you see your lovely clean hatch covers!

So far as I know, you're unlikely to find Boracol in your local chandlery, but a Google search brings it straight up. You want the 5R or 10R version. It's not cheap, but when you factor in the result and the time saved, it's not so dear after all.

DECK LEAKS

For many sailors, deck leaks are a fact of life. Any of us with boats dating from the plank-on-frame days almost certainly have one or two, usually in an impossible corner with no apparent source. Some have a whole lot more, especially if it's 80º Fahrenheit (27º Celsius) out there and the sky is baby-blue. The boat is drying out and unless she's a wonder of build and maintenance, she's probably opening up like a cauliflower. Here in the English Channel we dread the arrival of the inevitable thunderstorm sent over by the French because we know it's going to be tears, wet bunks and probably a dressing down from the lady of the ship as well.

I've had more than my share of disappointment from wooden decking, some of it legitimate from old pine boards spiked down onto deck beams that were always going to be too far apart. I learned to caulk decks the hard way, with oakum, irons and pitch. More recently, however, my sufferings have stemmed from decks laid on plywood with seams caulked with rubber that promised an end to all that. Let's take a look at rubber with no old-fashioned caulking underneath to keep the water out – a miracle

RIGHT: Gunning in the 'magic rubber' is a different world from the old days when hot pitch was poured from a ladle or a kettle, smoking as it ran into the seams

if applied well, a jade in the hands of the careless.

I had to discover a whole new set of techniques when the denizen of the quarter berth in a 'leak-free' yacht started to complain of a damp sleeping bag. I told him not to moan. A month later my wife held up a soggy pillow and indicated tell-tale brown streaks appearing on a number of deck beams. I knew them of old. With equity on the homestead for financing big jobs running low, it was time for action before the plywood sub-deck started to delaminate. Up in the fresh air, it was soon obvious that the rubber had been letting go on one side of the guilty seams, allowing ample access to the killer rainwater. I tried pulling the compound out. It wouldn't budge on the 'good' side and there were many, many feet to tackle. After cursing the builder, my fate and the hot weather in no particular order, I got up and gathered together a simple tool kit:

1. Stanley knife or heavy-duty scalpel to cut down the side of the seams *with greatest care so as not to damage the planking.*
2. A sharp ⅛ inch (3.2 mm) chisel to clean the last of the old rubber from the bottom of the seam.
3. A large roll of 120-grit sandpaper to fold into the seam and ream it out clean after the blades have finished.
4. A pensioned-off springy table knife with a round, spatulate blade end.
5. Several very expensive tubes of high-quality deck compound and a nice new gun.
6. Vitally important, the primer to go with the rubber.
7. Unlimited quantities of masking tape.
8. Ditto of old plastic bags to put the tape in when it's covered with liquid rubber.
9. Plenty of Latex gloves and some knee pads, both available from your local street market at attractive prices.
10. Some really old clothes you are willing to bin, because despite all your efforts to mitigate it, this is the filthiest job you will ever take on.
11. A few warm, sunny days – and good luck with that!

Given that we've revealed the equipment, the rest should be fairly obvious, but just for the record, this is what I've found works:

1. Down on your knees, Mate, in an attitude of prayer.
2. Gingerly slide the Stanley knife along the rubber/timber interface. If the grain is running at an angle, work 'down-grain' so that if the knife slips, it won't be guided away into the plank with horrid results.
3. When you've cut a good length away, take the thin-bladed chisel, bevel downwards, and run it under the rubber. This should now come out. If your luck's in, it won't be well attached and may strip by the yard. If not, keep on chiselling.
4. When you've a good few seams clear, sand them out and mask them carefully. At the extremity of each length of tape, turn the end back on itself for an inch or so to prevent it sticking to the wood. This is to give you something to get hold of. If you skimp on any of this, you'll wish you were dead in half an hour's time.
5. Prime the seam and do exactly what it says on the tin.
6. Gun in the compound, taking care to give a generous fill.
7. Run the table knife along the soft rubber to make sure it is pressed right down.
8. Stand by with the plastic bags, pick up one end of a strip of tape by the handle you gave it, and pull it away.
9. Stuff it in the bag. If you can manage this for a further 20 or so times without coating yourself and anybody else within a mile or two with hateful black goo, you can congratulate yourself. Once the stuff hits your skin or your best shirt, it's bye-bye happiness.
10. Admire your handiwork from afar. Remember not to walk on the wet seams for a day or so. Believe it or not, I and others have actually done this. The resulting language will surprise even you.

For those who insist on laid decks, the best alternative to this horror show is to get the job right in the first place, perhaps by insisting on full-depth seams. Alternatively, plump for traditional planking and deck beams. Pouring in hot pitch in the guise of Jeffery's Marine Glue after driving home the cotton is a harmless pleasure by comparison. It even smells better.

Who says progress is painless?

Traditional deck seams

Having owned antique wooden boats over a longer period of years than I'd like to admit, I've done more than my share of caulking, but the most important lesson time has taught me is that nobody ever knows it all. Among my personal collection of irons is a massive great thing with a business end, or 'blade' I suppose you'd call it, that measures the best part of 3/8 of an inch (9.5 mm) across. I picked this up in a blacksmith's yard in Nova Scotia where I was assured it had been used on the old fishing schooners. A vessel under my care in those days suffered from a seam just above the waterline that defied all sensible attempts to plim it up, but this mighty iron, suitably backed up with a supply of fresh, tarry oakum, saw her away to sea more or less safely.

Big seams never really frightened me after one yard foreman suggested caulking a nasty one with a welding rod. I only realised he was joking when he announced that the technique wasn't much good for the first year or so, but once the rod rusted in, it worked a treat.

At the other end of the scale, a different problem always arises and, until recently, I had notably failed to find an answer. Not so long since, I was called on to assist with the deck seams on a pre-war Harrison Butler yacht. Whether these were original or not, I couldn't tell, but they were so slim and delicate that my sharpest chinking iron struggled to drive in the cotton. We managed somehow, but the job wasn't convincing, so it was with deep joy that I finally found the solution. I was paying one of my regular visits to a favourite boatbuilder's workshop just down the road near my place. Every time I find myself propping up his work bench with a mug of tea in hand I seem to learn something new. On this occasion, I picked up a tool like a sort of small-diameter pizza cutter lying among the shavings, and asked what it was. The answer turned out to be what I'd been seeking for over 40 years and never found. It was a roller for caulking seams too slender for the most delicate iron in the average set, made from a narrow disc an inch or so in diameter let into the end of a handle that can be any size to suit you. Using it is a cinch. You lay the cotton along the seam and literally roll it in, leaning on the tool as hard as seems sensible. Its latest job had been on the Fife dayboat in the shed under restoration. It did a good job, because I couldn't discern any seams under the paint on her topsides. It would have been perfect for the decks on the old 'HB' that had baffled me.

Here's how to make one: the business end is a simple penny washer, but not just any penny washer. You need one of high-quality steel with a full diameter, the bigger the better, and only a tiny hole in the middle. If it's thin enough you won't need to grind down the edges, and in any case, you won't want it to be too sharp. The late Tristan Jones observed that he wouldn't have super-sharp knives on his boats and that if you couldn't see why there wasn't a lot he could do for you. This tool's a bit the same. All that's left once you have the 'wheel' is to find a suitable piece of hardwood somebody hasn't tidied up. Now shave and sand it into

LEFT: Caulking in the old-fashioned way. No gunning in rubber here. Every strike of the hammer drives more strength into the boat

shape to fit your hand, cut a notch in the end and drill through for a pin on which the washer can roll. Sometimes the simple ideas are the best.

POURING PITCH

Taken by and large, my wooden boats have done me pretty well, although none of them has been entirely without sin on the construction front. A case in point was *Hirta*, my Bristol Channel Pilot Cutter built by Janet Slade's lads on the beach in Polruan in 1911. Perhaps in the search for sailing performance, they went a bit light on the deck beams. The 50-foot boat was flush-decked and the full-width beams were spaced with the best part of three feet from one to the next. The result was that in 15 years of heavy use I was obliged to recaulk twice.

The planks were traditionally laid with a vee-seam for the cotton or oakum, topped off with pitch in the form of Jeffery's Marine Glue. While I had collected an excellent set of irons over the years, I never got round to kitting up with a proper pitch ladle. These days you can buy one new if you're lucky enough to have a spare hundred quid. Back then, your only hope was to find one in a marine bazaar; I never did. If you've a deck to caulk, you haven't struck lucky at the jumble and are disinclined to stump up a substantial sum, here, fresh from the School of Hard Knocks, is what I recommend you do:

Find an old kettle with a wide lid (discard this) and a good long spout with a proper swan-neck to it. Buy, beg or borrow a cheap one-ring camping stove. You could use the ship's galley, but things get into a bit of a mess after the first 300 feet of seam and the cook may add to your troubles by running berserk with a meat cleaver. Equip with a simple, disposable-cylinder gas torch. Produce a 5 foot x 5 foot square of heavy, old-fashioned canvas tarpaulin and steal a bendy spatula-ended table knife from the galley drawer. You'll also need a couple of flat blocks of wood suitable for standing a hot kettle on, to protect the tarp and give you somewhere to put the kettle down at the job.

Set up the stove on the tarp as near the first seam as you can; lever off the lid of the can of Jeffery's and beat the outside with a big hammer to break up the pitch which is, of course, solid at this stage. Drop the bits into the kettle to about 2/3 full. Light the gas ring on medium heat and while the pitch is melting, mask up the seams you are going to pour. Use extra-wide tape that virtually covers the whole plank by the time you've masked the seams on both sides.

Now go back to the kettle. Be very careful to achieve readiness for a perfect flow without letting the black potion boil. The pockets of escaping solvents ruin its consistency and wreck the result. I recently watched some guy on a TV documentary pouring boiling, bubbling pitch into the seams of a deck. If the yard foreman who monitored my early efforts had seen this, the poor chap would have been held up to public scorn. The pitch is ready when it has the liquidity of warmed-up golden syrup. Give the spout of the kettle a quick blast with the blowlamp to save the pitch from cooling as it pours, then take it to the seam. Put the kitchen knife in your pocket.

Kneel at the seam and carefully pour in the fluid pitch. You'll be surprised how easily it runs in to start with. As it cools the process will slow down. Human nature being what it is, you won't stop pouring now as you should. Instead, you'll keep going until finally, a half-set dribble doesn't quite make it to the seam, which should be filled to a modest overflow. Nip back and put the kettle on the heat once more.

The pitch in the seam will still be pliable. The really good hot stuff will have taken care of itself, but there's a fair chance the warm, gloopy end of things may not have quite reached the oakum to complete the job. This is where you whip out your kitchen knife and run it along the seam, pressing down to force any reluctant pitch in to where it ought to be. You can now pull off the tape to reveal a reasonably neat job. It might not pass muster on the narrow, swept planks of a gold-plater, but it'll be fine for a working boat, even a smart one.

If you want to be really traditional, you'll forget the masking tape and let the pitch run over the deck on both sides of the seam. Leave it for a few weeks while the passing traffic tramples it in, then scrape it off with a shipyard scraper. A grisly business, but it is effective, so you pays your money and hopes for the best...

STOPPING UP

Once a seam in a plank-on-frame wooden boat has been caulked with cotton or oakum, the final stage in keeping out the water is the stopping. I'll never forget tackling this job on my 50-foot pilot cutter. She'd just been caulked afresh by Alastair Garland at The Elephant Boatyard on the Hamble River. I wasn't the world's worst caulker by any means, but the boat had been suffering a chronic, undiscoverable leak and I felt that handing the job to a professional might give her a better chance. The leak itself is not the main event here, and when Alastair had clinked his irons back into their bag and sloped off to sort out someone else's problems, I was left with stopping her up. I didn't dare work out how many feet of seam I had to face, but I know now that it had to be the thick end of 2,000, so my usual cobble-up of stopping material wasn't going to cut the mustard. I needed the right stuff, so I went to ask the yard foreman, a proper prophet if ever there was one.

He presented me with a 15-inch (38 cm) square of half-inch (12.7 mm) WBP plywood, a jumbo-sized tub of fresh linseed oil putty and a bag of red lead powder.

'You guard that powder well, boy,' he warned, 'And don't let any policemen see it.' He'd had a hard time coming to terms with modern health and safety regulations and so potent was the lead content that he'd convinced himself it must be illegal. He showed me how to pile a wodge of putty onto the board after warming it up by rolling it in his hands. Then he made a hollow in the middle and shook in a carefully unmeasured portion of the precious powder. Finally, he mixed it all up using a single-edged putty knife to create a heavy red paste of a creamy consistency so divine I was tempted to eat it. I'd already primed the seams as directed by the great man. The knife shoved the putty in sweetly, then compressed it with the flex of its blade so that, as it drew away, the stopping bulged ever so slightly from the seam to indicate that it was well and truly filled. I must have recharged the board 100 times before I was finished, but the result looked good and held up well as the years went by.

It doesn't matter what job you're doing on a traditional boat, there's always some tooth-sucking Job's comforter strolls up uninvited to tell you you're doing it all wrong. In this case, it was a bearded individual in a tattered smock who delivered the free advice that anyone who knew anything stopped his bottom seams with red lead putty but used white lead for his topsides. By this time I'd probably knifed the wondrous confection into a quarter-mile of seam and was not in the mood for confrontation. I thanked him, ignored him and finished the task. Later, I reported his remarks to the foreman.

'Oh,' he said. 'That old chestnut. Well, I s'pose if you're wanting to paint your yacht white and put her into a concours and you're too mean to give her the full primer, brush cement, undercoats, and several topcoats, you might just get a bit of leech-through to spoil your job. White lead would solve that, but it'd go hard sooner than the red, and then you'd have cracked seams and be sorry. On your boat, he's talking rubbish.'

And he was. The job never failed above or below the waterline. The leak didn't stop either, but that is another story.

MAINTAINING BRIGHTWORK

Once upon a time I sailed a smart boat that had varnished ash blocks. They looked great at first, pale in colour and made a nice contrast with the golden pine spars, but as time went by they took a few knocks and it was a different story. They suffered those small dings inevitable when you actually go sailing. The rain and salt slipped under the edge of the abrasions and the lovely blocks began to show horrid black stains. If I'd had nothing else to do with my life, I could have carefully patched the varnish as soon as it was damaged but, as with most of us, there were a number of real-world reasons why this didn't happen. First, I was too busy sailing to notice every knock. Secondly, even if I did, I simply hadn't the time to feather

BELOW: Stopping up with red lead putty might look easy, but it's the twist of the wrist as the blade pushes home with its flex supplying the pressure that makes the difference

back the edge of each scar with medium-grade sandpaper, apply two carefully mixed coats of 50/50 varnish/thinners, followed a day or two later with several coats of rubbed-down full-strength over the gap; then, finally, a proper rub-down of the whole block and a coat overall. You see what I mean. All this is a long way from ideal in the rough-and-tumble of trying to go for a sail at the weekend. Varnish, I decided, had its limitations.

Things were better where the wood treated was an easier colour, such as teak or mahogany. Oak, however, tended to fall into the same category as ash. I also noted that if a varnished surface didn't get interfered with and was well done in the first place, it would often last a season or even more without visitation. I was starting to build up a picture. Then I went ocean sailing and took a loud wake-up call. The blocks were hammered far more severely than ever they were in the Solent, and don't even mention the bowsprit! The tropics seemed to have a private store of 120-grit sandpaper for stripping spars. It'd had a good seven coats of 'Spinnaker', but a trade-wind crossing left it in a sorry state. I patched it as best I could, then tackled the North Atlantic for a home run. It was half bare when I landed in Ireland from Nova Scotia and I'd about had it with varnish.

The next summer I sailed to Norway, where I found the beginnings of an answer. Rather than varnish, the guys up there were anointing their brightwork with pine tar oil. They thinned the first few coats with raw turpentine – the real thing, not a 'substitute' – then whacked on as many top coats as they had time for. No rubbing down was needed and the results weren't half bad. It had to be said that the surfaces to which the oil was applied were generally a little short of the finest gloss finish, so you couldn't expect too much, but I was impressed nonetheless.

I acquired a 5-gallon drum of this unction for remarkably little outlay and laid it onto my suffering bowsprit, my more vulnerable blocks, and the oak capping on my bulwarks after scraping them clean of residual varnish. It didn't look quite as good as the yacht varnish did when the seventh coat was fresh out of the can, but it lasted far better. And here's the crunch: when it took a knock, patching it was dead easy. A quick clean-up with sandpaper – and I do mean quick – followed by a few 50/50s and a topcoat with no rubbing down. You couldn't see where I'd been.

I was now well on the way to a solution for brightwork on a boat that is worked hard, but there remained the fact that the original Norwegian oil wasn't really designed for yacht finish. I rubbed along with this for years until the monster can finally ran out. Then my long-term shipmate Pol Bergius began importing a more refined Norwegian product which he called 'Varnol'. This, if used carefully as described on the can, could generate a finish as good as most amateurs can achieve with a varnish brush. It carried the benefits of very little work once the wood had been prepared, and great 'patchability'. In fact, it was so non-labour intensive that, so long as the substrate was in good condition, all that was needed for a new season was to rub it with a cloth soaked in real turps, let it dry, then brush on a fresh coat.

All good things come to an end, however, and when I could no longer source Varnol, I was obliged to visit the chandlery to try my luck with Owatrol's commercial version known as Deks Olje, 'D1' and 'D2'. I'd heard mixed reports about this as one does for any system, but after my experience with the real thing I took the trouble to read the instructions. Following them to the letter produced results that are not far short of any you'll see outside of a factory varnish finish or an expensive professional job.

So here's the policy that came out of all this mixed experience: any brightwork that is not under pressure from weather or getting knocked, such as coachroof sides or hatch coamings well clear of the sea, is treated to the traditional varnish experience. It lasts well and it does look great. Blocks that fly around, toerails that suffer fender lanyards and big feet, cockpit coamings that are chafed by sheets and bottoms, all get the Deks Olje option, as do bowsprits. And the good news is that the old trick of cutting back the gloss with the turps still works, which saves sandpaper and a deal of hard work.

After a decade of the Deks Olje treatment, my once-sorry pine bowsprit went a deep, dark golden colour that looked gorgeous. One or two darker marks where I hadn't quite got the patching right just blended in. Many of our boats are far from new, and there's beauty in maturity wrought by the years that's often missed when striving after a different idea of perfection.

BELOW: Oil or varnish? It's a serious question with two good answers, depending on the work the wood will do and the conditions to which it will be subjected

VARNISH IN THE WINTER

As a frugal mariner who pays his own bills I hate to say this, but if you want total happiness from your varnishing, it pays to buy a new can each season. If funds are tight and you still have 3/4 of this year's can left in the autumn, all is not lost. So long as it's kept at a moderate temperature it should survive. Before leaving it though, be sure to shake the can upside down for a few seconds so the varnish runs down inside and covers the joint around the lid. Flip it back up again and it's perfectly airtight. Don't leave it in the fo'c'sle either. It can get cold in there. Take it home and pop it under the spare bed. With luck, nobody will notice, and if it's a bit on the thick side in spring, thin it carefully with Owatrol. Accept no substitute.

WOODEN BLOCKS – MAINTAINING PERFORMANCE

A quality wooden block will last the life of a yacht or boat. When the pilot cutter *Hirta* passed from my ownership in the mid-1990s she still carried a number of elm blocks dating from 1911. Several had patent sheaves showing signs of age. Others favoured simple sheave-on-pin arrangements. Some pins were worn, but not dangerously so. A few had been replaced, but all were serviceable. We sailed the 35-ton cutter thousands of ocean miles with no winches and only an average muscle count, so it would have been wretched if the blocks hadn't worked as they should. What follows are some random thoughts on making sure that they never let us down.

TYPES OF BLOCK

Regardless of sheave numbers, beckets, strops and other variables, wooden blocks come in three main types: a sheave running on a steel pin with no other bearings, an old-fashioned patent sheave with roller bearings around the centre to bear on the pin, and modern sheaves of bronze or plastic running on a stainless steel pin. A refinement is an oilite bush impregnated with lubricant pressed into the centre of a bronze sheave.

SERVICING

When was the last time you noticed a set of blocks 'clacking' as you hoisted the gaff or sweated in your sheets? In case you don't know, that's the sound of patent sheaves whose bearings have stuck in one place and whose pins have worn. As the rollers are forced unwillingly over the resulting 'flat' on the pin, they clatter as they go. The friction is awful and it all happens through lack of basic maintenance. Yet looking after wooden blocks is one of the least onerous jobs on a boat. I actually enjoy it so much that I made a video about it and put it up on YouTube, just for fun (https://youtube.com/watch?v=ntBT2xCq58Q). Like the jolly plumber in California whose little film showed me how to fix my domestic toilet flush, nobody paid me. I did it for what Julius Caesar once called 'the general good'. The block I used was a hefty one with three

RIGHT: Stripping and servicing blocks that have been regularly looked after is a pleasant job on a winter's night

patent sheaves that was handed to me almost 40 years ago by a fellow pilot-boat owner. It was too heavy for his boat. I had the same problem, so I carted it home and used it as a doorstop. By the time it made its first public appearance on the internet it was oiled to yacht standard, but in all those years I hadn't stripped it down. If you've never tried it, here's how it works:

- Get your tools together. For a big block you'll need a heavy hammer, a drift, a container big enough to hold a sheave comfortably, some paraffin (kerosene), and a retired toothbrush. If the pin has a cover over one or both ends, you'll probably also need a suitable screwdriver. A few absorbent rags are a must.

- Inspect the block. If it has a traditional pin, one end will be square to stop it turning, and the other round. There may be a plate over the square end. If so, unscrew it and put it on one side. The late Harry Spencer of Cowes used 'ship ha'pennies' for this, and very handsome they were. Other pricey units have various logos, but a simple brass disc is sufficient to make sure the pin can't come out. Workaday blocks have no cover at all.

- The pin is now driven out by hitting the round end with the hammer and drift. You'll have to set the block shell up on some sort of frame to allow the pin to drop down as you drive it. It's easy for me because my bench has a removable section perfect for this job. A 'Workmate' mini-bench will do the same trick, but if all else fails, a strong plastic beer crate or a couple of heavy wooden chocks work fine.

- As you hit the pin, it will talk to you. If the sound is a thick, dull 'thunk', it's starting to drive out and all is well. When the hammer bounces with a sort of 'chink' noise, it's bad news. The pin is not for moving and you'll have to whack it a bit harder. Unless the block is a hopeless case, it will succumb in the end to a dedicated effort.

- The pin will be caked in old grease. Submerge it in the paraffin bath and give it a good clean with the toothbrush, then wipe it on a rag and take a critical look. With luck it will show little sign of wear and be ready to go back. If the sheave bearings have been sticking you may find one side worn down. Classic block pins are usually way over-size for strength, so if the wear is not too bad you can reset the pin the other way up so that the side taking the load from the sheave is pristine. Ideally, you'll replace the pin, but unless your local marine junk store happens to have one with a square end that fits, you're on a hiding to nothing. In extremis, I've been known to find myself a steel pin of the right size to drive in, fabricate a cover for what should have been the square end if it doesn't already have one, and hope for the best. Blocks cobbled up like this have crossed the North Atlantic without mishap, so 'nothing ventured, nothing gained'.

- Now, the sheaves. Some don't have patent bearings, so just clean them and inspect for wear. Where the holes are really pear-shaped, take them to your local engineer to have them bushed, but this is rare.

- Patent sheaves are a delight. The centre of the sheave carries a cage containing roller bearings. These cuddle up to the pin and run sweetly until the grease, which invariably has been over-enthusiastically applied, solidifies and stops them turning. Paraffin and the dear old toothbrush clean this assembly up easily. Dry it with the rags and you're ready to go. If the bearing cage is breaking up from age and neglect, perhaps you'll have to dig deep for a new block and consign the mortal remains to the snuggery wall in the 'Bosun's Rest (fine ales and spirits, licensee, Black Jake)'.

- Oiling block shells that take a hammering is better than varnishing them, and the ideal time for this is when the pins and sheaves are out. I used to hang all 55 from my last gaff cutter on lines strung round the back of my workshop. They were a brave sight swinging in the breeze and we could get coat after coat on them undisturbed – so long as we chose our weather.

- Reassembly is simple. A light smear of waterproof grease on the pin. If the bearings are worn, use lanolin for the cage to help take up any slack. Slip the pin back in and drive the square end firmly but kindly home, until flush with the shell. Replace any cover plate and that's it. Do this every year or two and, no matter how young you may be, a set of traditional blocks will see you out.

Painting the Roof-top

Boot tops and wale strakes

The boot top is that critical line painted fore-and-aft just above the waterline. If it's a classy job, it might be picked out in a different colour to the bottom paint and the topsides. Where budgets are tight, a boat may have no boot top at all, merely a defined interface between antifouling and the topside enamel nicely above the load waterline, but whichever it is, that line tells us things about an owner that his partner probably never knew.

Check out the drawings of a pre-war design from the board of Dr Harrison Butler. You'll notice that the boot-top line is plotted on his plans, and you can't miss the fact that it is definitely not parallel sided. Its upper edge describes a shallow parabola whose arc lies part-way between the flat, lower waterline and the springing sheer of her toerail. Harrison Butler's boats were typically around 26 feet, so the difference between his curving boot top and one drawn with a straight edge is little more than an inch or two at most, yet it brings the yacht to life.

Now take a stroll around your local yard and look carefully. Modern boot tops are almost invariably painted parallel to the water and they kill a yacht's looks stone dead. If the poor vessel has no sheer to speak of, the designer hasn't much choice. Neither does the painter, because a curving boot top under a flat deck would look ludicrous.

Where the boat has a kick to her profile as she should have, a touch of movement in the boot top works wonders.

Scribing a proper boot top is a tricky, specialised business. It lies well beyond my expertise, so if yours needs cheering up, find a time-served man. If they've all disappeared from your foreshore, dig a proper yacht painter out of retirement and slip him an old-fashioned ten-shilling note. He'll probably do the job just for the joy of showing the world that people still can.

WALE STRAKES

An inch makes the difference, too, when it comes to painted sheer strakes and wale strakes tacked onto fibreglass or epoxy replicas. A plank-on-frame construction with a wale strake would have a board built into the hull that's a bit beefier than its neighbours, with a nice rounded edge. Originally of practical function, these embellishments cheat the eye and make the vessel appear lower-slung and maybe a bit sexier than she actually is. The technique is honourable in replicas for aesthetic purposes, yet the original wooden boat seems always to look so much better.

I was contemplating this question one day down in Cornwall when the late Martin Heard of Gaffers and Luggers put me straight. The reason is, he said, that if the 'bolt-on' wale or painted 'sheer strake' is parallel sided, which most are, the builder hasn't thought it through. A plank-on-frame or clinker boat normally sees her strakes tapered towards the ends. The paint line or the shape of the wale strake was defined by this taper and, however slight it was, it lifted the eye by subtly following the sheer. The whole boat was enhanced. If we just slap on

LEFT: Martyn has shown us a really large yacht of the classic variety having her boot top painted. What skill it must have taken to mark up this giant trim line that gives the boat so much life!

a parallel line or bolt on a handy board after knocking the corners off and rounding the ends, the effect is often the opposite.

COVE LINES

A bit of thought over this finishing touch can harvest a big result. Most traditional wooden yachts have a cove line cut into the top strake, making painting or applying gold leaf relatively simple. Whether it carries the glorious Fife dragon or simply fades discreetly away, it will enhance the yacht's lines many times over. If there's no physical guide for the brush, the position and nature of the cove line is down to the painter. I had a boat once with black topsides and a yellow painted cove line six inches or so below the deck, terminating in an arrow-head forward and a point aft. It looked great, breaking up the expanse of black and, by cheating the eye, it created an impression that the topsides were lower than they actually were. A piece of art.

In a modern fibreglass hull, the builder must decide on the cove line. Sadly, not all of today's producers have served a seven-year apprenticeship with an old-fashioned master yacht painter. One much-admired modern classic series has a sheer which, to the observant connoisseur, is too flat aft. Beneath it, the cove line follows this virtual straight edge, ending with a flourish which broadens on its lower side. The effect drags the eye downwards as if in sorrow. Had the flourish been the other way up, it would have lifted the gaze and disguised an otherwise excellent yacht's lack of sheer.

If in doubt, mock it up first on a profile drawing. You'll see the effect straight away.

BOATS IN WINTER

There's much to be said for laying up ashore. If you can push the boat into a shed, you're in Fat City with the varnish protected until spring and no worries about deck leaks. It's pricey though, and many yards simply don't have it on offer. One benefit of putting the boat inside is that the stick must come out. Even if she's in the open, a mast that is pulled every year should never give any problems because you can treat it to a free annual survey.

MAST OUT

I couldn't afford a shed in my wooden boat days, but I used to lift the mast every other winter. It was a policy that served me well. Modern mast racks are designed for tin sticks. There's not a lot to be done with these on an annual basis, so riggers tend to rack them up so close that you can't get a cigarette paper between them. If you don't say anything to the yard, a wooden spar often ends up stuffed in among this lot, rammed hard against Joe Soap's radar scanner with Fred Bloggs' manky old headfoil draped across the spreaders. Let this happen and you'll do well to get near it, let alone go over it inch by inch, rub it down, check the track fastenings, sort out that sticky burgee halyard sheave and tap around the hounds with the ship's toffee hammer, heart in mouth, listening for the soggy 'thunk' of rot. Buy the rigger a beer, cross his palm

RIGHT: Coming up for the winter. Tidying up and stripping down, ready to put on the covers

with paper, say nice things about his kids, do whatever you need to, but make him love you so that when you ask him to give you some fighting room, he nods understandingly and finds a way. It really makes a difference.

ROT HOTSPOTS

Wooden spars left rigged for years are a happy hunting ground for wet rot. I've seen my share of this, including the ultimate sinking feeling when my screwdriver disappeared into the hounds up to its handle. Of course, the hounds can be checked from a bosun's chair, but there's no substitute for having a good prod with the mast on trestles.

Mast partners are another favourite rot spot. The softwood can be compressed by the wedges leaving the fibres vulnerable, the coat may leak, especially in winter when there's nobody sleeping in the saloon to complain about it, the dreaded rain water gets trapped and away we go. You can sniff around all you like in the season, but the only way to be sure is to have the mast out.

The step is the third hiding place for misery. Is it dry when the tenon lifts out?

Yes? Joy! Go directly to the pub and celebrate.

No? Find out why, clear its limbers, dry it, soak it in Stockholm tar and make sure it never happens again. I once left this too long. The wretch of a dodgy step ran under cabin bulkheads and replacing it was an epic that moulded my character in ways I wouldn't care to repeat. The end product, though, provided a lovely dry spot to slip a King's shilling, and to be doubly sure there was no recurrence I drilled the step and inserted Boron rods.

Where the tenon on the mast has gone soft, dry it thoroughly and re-inspect after a few weeks. With luck it'll be dry and a bit fibrous, giving you the option to try your hand with some thin epoxy or a graving piece. If this doesn't sound like your bag, call in the experts. As you click the mouse to clobber the bank account, be grateful you didn't leave the spar in for another year.

IDLE MACHINERY

Nearly all of us have an engine these days. Engines love work. They don't get any when the boat's laid up, so what to do?

If the boat's going to be ashore, the penultimate task is to change the lubricating oil and filter. Old oil contains acid ingredients and sludge that degrade an idle engine, whether it's a modern diesel or an important museum piece. Get rid of the stuff and give the machine a chance.

Since you are going to that trouble, why not change the fuel filters at the same time, and do what needs to be done with the gearbox oil too. Whether the boat is stored ashore or afloat, if she's outside, or even inside in an unheated shed, the fuel in the tanks will be subject to big temperature and humidity changes. Any air above the fuel will carry moisture in it, replenished via the tank breathers. An abrupt fall in temperature condenses this and that's a few more drops of the dreaded water in your diesel. Pressing the tanks up full at lay-up time is the best way around this. The less air in the top of the tank, the less water in the diesel next year and, of course, you've taken the hit in the wallet six months ago, not when you're having to stump up for antifouling, a new sail and all the rest of the new-season commitments.

What about antifreeze? There's no issue

about the inner cooling system freezing because it should already be filled with coolant to the manufacturer's spec, but what about the raw water? Even in areas where there's little danger of residual brine freezing, the issue of corrosion remains. Antifreeze protects against this as well as keeping things liquid at low temperatures so, before hauling the boat, the last job goes like this:

- Buy a gallon of eco-antifreeze and mix it 50/50 with tap water in your garden watering can. Two gallons of this is sufficient for the job on most engines up to around 55HP. Now add a squirt of 'Wild Green Fairy' or some more ecological detergent as a tell-tale.
- Shut the engine-cooling seacock.
- Open the lid of the raw-water strainer.
- Start the engine and give it a few revs.
- As soon as the level in the strainer drops, top it up with the antifreeze mix. Keep pouring until it's all gone or until your mate on the dock reports suds in the exhaust.
- Shut down the engine promptly and replace the strainer cover.

The engine is now not only proof against freezing, the heat exchanger and exhaust elbow are thoroughly lubricated and no creeping salt build-up will degrade them before next spring. Warp the boat into the lift and forget your troubles.

An engine laid up afloat can be treated in the same way if it won't be run at all. However, perhaps a happier solution is to make a pact with oneself to visit the vessel at least once a fortnight and run the motor under load for an hour or so each time. Running it in neutral gear is bad news because it will take ages to warm up and diesels love to work. Too much of this will cause deterioration to the cylinder bores among other things so, if she's alongside, make sure the stern line and the head spring are well set up, then select ahead and give it half revs. The engine will enjoy its outing and the batteries will love a good old jolt from the alternator. I always managed the time for this, so my preference was to change the oil, then run the engine up while freshening the nips on the lines or the mooring to prevent chafe. The engine was always ready for service as I carried the gaff and boom back aboard in time for Easter.

FROZEN SEACOCKS

One frosty afternoon I'd been wrestling in my bilge for an hour or more trying to withdraw the tapered barrel of a Blake's seacock. It had jammed solid on the old grease and although I'd tried all I knew to move it, the wretched thing hadn't given a fraction of a millimetre on which to pin my hopes. On the edge of despair I was slumped beneath the boat having a smoke, as one did in those happier times, when the yard foreman appeared. How he knew what my problem was I have no idea, but he strolled over and handed me a long, heavy screwdriver. 'Here you are, Nipper,' he said. 'Shove that up the spout from the outside where we are now and hit it with a hammer.' I did. At the first swing of the maul the seized bronze broke its grip and the seacock clattered into my bilge, as clean as a whistle. Try it. It never fails.

Proper job — dealing with the unlikely

Textbooks on boat repair and maintenance tell us how to do a proper job, and there's no arguing with that. Modern courses are often helpful too, but the old seven-year apprenticeship taught all the official skills and more. Because the lad was with his master through thick and sometimes very thin, he learned to think outside the box from time to time. For the sailor who hasn't had the benefit of serving his time, the wits he was born with are sometimes all he has, but to use them, he must be shipmates with a well-stocked bosun's locker. Keeping the ancient unctions of the sea to hand is vital. You never know when you'll need them. It goes without saying that a full tool kit, a comprehensive screw-box and a supply of bolts, nuts, washers and boat nails are basic essentials, but so is developing the habit of picking up odd bits of hardware you find lying around in the dust of the boatyard. The most unlikely junk can be pressed into service in extremis, and one great thing about traditional craft is that, in many cases, displacement is on the heavy side. This means that a few extra pounds of scrap metal tucked away low down in a dry corner awaiting their moment in the sun won't be noticed.

One occasion when all this apparently dodgy advice stood me in good stead took

BELOW: The 'bullet-proof' steering gear on *Hirta*, my 1911 pilot cutter, salvaged in the 1950s from another hefty cutter

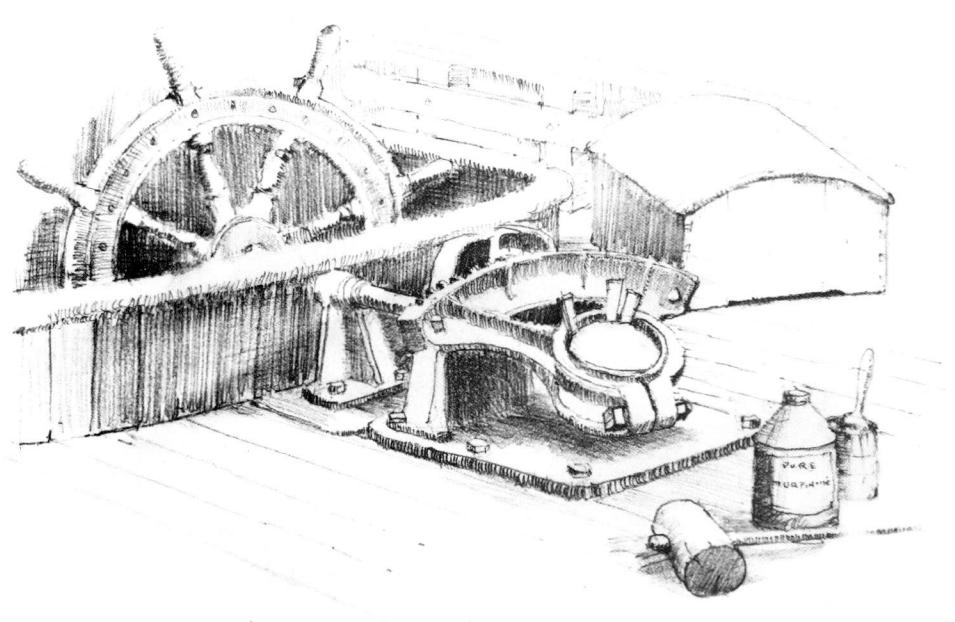

place when sailing my 35-ton cutter in the tropics. Her wooden rudder stock came up through the deck in its trunk at the forward end of the counter. An iron ring was clamped around the upper end of the stock with a toothed quadrant mounted on its forward face. This connected by a simple system of bevelled gears to the wheel. The stock head and all the gear except the wheel were covered by a beautiful teak box with a lid whose curved top matched that of the companionway. Very elegant and totally functional. This set-up, regularly lubricated with lanolin from the bosun's stores and engine oil from a well-loved old can, never missed a trick in 15 years. The only problem developed when the dry heat cooked the ancient timber of the head of the stock. It was far too 'mature' for even the smartest wood buffs to guess what tree it came from, but oak or elm were the front runners. Whatever it was, the heat shrank the wood as it expanded the iron collar, creating a gap so severe that the stock began slopping around. There was no thread left to take up on the clamp bolt and, suddenly, my bulletproof steering started to look vulnerable.

WHAT TO DO?

Luckily, among my store of quality hardwoods that all classics should surely carry, I found a length of what we used to call 'shaky deal'. This was rubbishy softwood full of cracks, only good for house-builders' shuttering. How it ended up among the teak and purple heart I've no idea, but it saved the day when the classier products would have stood no chance. What was required was something to wedge the collar tight that would simply disintegrate if and when the stock swelled once more. The deal was just the job. I cut a series of long thin wedges, pared them down with a sharp chisel then carefully drove them into the gap all round the stock. The movement stopped, but it couldn't last.

We had to persuade the stock to swell back to its proper size and this is where the bosun's stores came in. On the shelf stood linseed oil and Stockholm tar, both nice and fluid in the 90º Fahrenheit (32º Celsius) swelter. They'd feed the wood with good things and, as it absorbed them, their own volume would seep into the heart of the suffering timber, giving it new life, but even at these temperatures they weren't about to soak in very fast. The adjacent paint locker held the answer. There, I found a gallon of real raw turpentine, kept for thinning the Norwegian Deks Olje I used on my spars. The stuff would dissolve the tar and it would thin the linseed too. I mixed it all up in a tub and brushed it onto the rudder stock. The wedges sucked it in as though they were dying of thirst. The hardwood which had been scraped clean to expose the end grain, took somewhat longer, but repeated applications finally did the trick. My shaky deal was crushed into non-existence and the rudder stock plimmed up lovely. It never wobbled in its collar again.

I should perhaps apologise for this long story in a slim volume supposed to be crammed with handy tips for the ship's husband or wife, but on reflection I do not. Those of us who go down to the sea in vernacular craft never know what unlikely challenges will present themselves. Without a carefully cultivated bosun's locker and a fair supply of items we may never need, what could be an easy repair may end up as an impossibility. At sea it's always down to us and what we have to hand. Out there beyond the range of VHF, there's no AA.

USEFUL MATERIALS

WAX FOR HAPPINESS

Kicking around in every well-stuffed bosun's bag you'll find a fragrant lump of beeswax. It will be scored by all the lengths of spunyarn and sail twine that the bosun's stripped across its corners to confer strength and substance, to help it render and to make threading his needles a piece of cake. These days you can buy waxed twine in the local chandlers, and very good some of it is too, but a lot of what we end up with is not waxed and more's the pity. Sail and whipping twine comes in two varieties now. There's the usual round stuff that's laid up and offered in various sizes, often unwaxed. It has its uses, but for a palm-and-needle whipping or a small-scale serving, you can't beat the flat variety. It slips into the needle eye almost by itself and, if you're careful not to twist it laying on the turns, you get a lovely clean result. It also lends itself to doubling up. Having threaded the needle, halve the length at the eye, tie the ends together (optional) and pass both parts with each turn. This means half as many whipping turns and only a single round of frappings to finish off.

You can buy block beeswax on the internet, but divers use it to lube their drysuit zips, so the dive store should have some ready to go.

GOOD-QUALITY NAILS

It's all very well shipping out with a locker stocked to bursting with quality fastenings. You never know when you'll need them of course, but it's a mistake to turn your back on more mundane fixings because you're sailing a smart yacht. Years ago my tiller snapped at the rudder head in a North Atlantic storm. I chiselled out the remains from the rudder head and shoved what was left of it back in the hole. The only way to secure it was with six-inch (15 cm) hot-dipped galvanized nails from my bosun's bag. I whacked them in, then bent the ends over. It didn't look great, but it got me home. A recent eBay search revealed 13 for £3.90, plus £2 postage. Bargain. Better 'buy it now'!

RUSTY FASTENINGS

Iron's good stuff for fastening boats. It's strong, it's cheap and workboats were held together with it for centuries. Unfortunately, even with years of useful life ahead of it, rust tends to sneak in. If the red menace can get out past the bungs, a little weep goes a long way to ruin a boat's beauty and her owner's reputation. Refastening is rarely a realistic option, but help is at hand. Old-fashioned muriatic acid eats rust more effectively than any store-bought compound in a plastic bottle. Slip on the rubber gloves and goggles, wipe it on, watch the rust disappear, rinse copiously, step back, and enjoy your lovely boat. You only need a tiny bit for rust on paint, so damage and eco-problems are not an issue, but do rinse well and early.

RIGHT: No rusty fastenings on this fine yacht. She'll be held together with bronze!

CHAPTER SEVEN
SEAMANSHIP

More than once I have been asked to define seamanship. When one starts to add up all the 1,001 skills that make up the thoroughgoing seaman, it becomes clear that it can't be done in terms of specifics. It's more subtle than that, and a lot simpler. If you read the narrative books about cruising written by the pioneer ocean sailor Eric Hiscock, you start to think that nothing dramatic ever seems to happen to the great man at sea. Storms are made light work, navigation seems largely just to happen, gear failure is a rarity. It is only when you study his technical books about how to set a yacht up for a circumnavigation that you begin to understand how he and his wife Susan managed to make their voyages with so little fuss. Their attention to well-thought-out bosun's work is meticulous, and as they continue on their seemingly endless way in boats tiny by today's standards, we see how the policy pays off. There was nothing flashy about the Hiscocks. They were just supreme seamen.

The definition of seamanship, it seems to me, is that every manoeuvre, every knot and splice, every tactical decision, is made to look easy. Sailing with skippers who are good seamen is totally relaxing because you know that whatever wickedness the weather or the sea is cooking up, they are always one step ahead. They see trouble coming before it shows itself and they're ready for it with a plan in place.

The seamanship considered in this section of the book is an eclectic mix and most of it is really bosun's work. How to swig a heavy halyard is a long way from sculling a dinghy with a single oar; hoisting a fisherman anchor to a bulwark stow may seem a different discipline from deciding how a burton purchase is to be rigged, but all are part of the seaman's art.

In the end, seamanship is the beating heart of what we do. Our pride, and our delight.

RIGHT: Towing along sweetly, but how far up or down the stem is the painter's attachment point? The answer is pure seamanship and if it is ignored, the boat will tow like a haystack

Towing dinghies in a following sea

Now that I sail a 'modern classic', I can no longer ship a decent stem dinghy or a nice Nordic pram, so I have signed on with the hordes condemned to limp ashore with the wet bottom that awaits all those who travel in inflatables. A real dinghy on the other hand is a joy, but when cruising between anchorages there is always the temptation to tow it rather than suffer the relative hassle of heaving it up on deck. This idleness, it must be said at the outset, creates a problem that really has no satisfactory solution.

The grim payoffs are twofold. Even reaching, the drag from the painter can take a knot off the speed of a 30-foot yacht. Close-hauled, the effect on performance is little short of brutal, but it's running in a seaway when the second downside really snarls. The yacht, of course, will surge and slow as the waves pick her up. The dinghy does the same and all may go well for a while until, if your luck is out, the two motions decide not to coincide. The punt then comes surfing along with a slack bight of painter waiting to snap back into line on the next wave. This is when the line breaks, or perhaps drags the towing ring out of the stem. Not good, but worse is in store when, instead of surging up alongside, it stays bang in line and either smashes into the yacht's transom or climbs unceremoniously into the cockpit. I've had both experiences. I've also had a dinghy break loose in a huge swell off the west coast of Ireland in a large gaff cutter and enjoyed a lively afternoon recovering it. You'd think I'd learn, wouldn't you, but despite the considerable sum of this experience I have no oven-ready answer, other than to suggest adjusting the length of the tow to suit the sea state. In search of enlightenment, I have turned to a higher authority and opened my 1939 copy of Francis B Cooke.

Cooke first considers the possibility of towing a bucket astern of the dinghy. In his day, buckets were galvanized iron with handles built for sterner stuff than the pathetic apologies one often finds in the new millennium. All is not lost, however, and the better chandlers offer stout, undersized rubber buckets with handles well up to the job to the discerning shopper. One of these will certainly discourage the dreaded surfing, but by definition it will add even more to the drag the small boat is already exerting. For a sailor with ambitions of arriving before closing time this is therefore an unattractive option.

Cooke sailed yachts too small even to think about carrying the punt on deck, so he had plenty of practice. His best answer surprised me, but one can only speak as one finds and it worked for him. First, he made sure the dinghy was properly trimmed for towing. I've noted this myself and it means either carrying a little extra weight in the stern to keep the tiny skeg well down, or towing from a fitting near the waterline. This will have the effect of raising the stem a little which, of course, is what the doctor ordered. Weight in the bow is a disaster.

Next, he recommends towing 'short' from two lines, one from each of the yacht's quarters. In moderate conditions this works well, but when the big seas start rolling up astern and things are looking leery, he has an answer. A warp 10 fathoms long streamed from the dinghy provides enough drag to hold her in line most of the time, without trying to pull the stern off the hood ends. When not needed, this is attached to the dinghy's transom and brought aboard the yacht where it is coiled ready to deploy by simply tossing it overboard. In Cooke's day, small yachts generally didn't have engines, so wrapping the line up in your own or someone else's propeller when arriving after dark wasn't an issue. It is today, so go for a floating warp and watch out!

The honest fisherman

The honest fisherman. No such thing? You might have a point, except that we're not talking about the chap quietly attending to his pots or the midnight trawler skipper protected by the Colregs and his green-over-white who alters course across our bows. The sort of fisherman that should be of interest to all classic boaters isn't out there terrorising the pelagic population, it's the anchor that bears his name.

A hundred years ago, fisherman anchors were standard issue on yachts and small commercial craft. Today, their reputation has been besmirched and they are often missing altogether from lists of desirable ground tackle in yachting textbooks, which is a pity. The first reason for this disappearance is the understandable though erroneous conclusion that, compared with modern patent anchors, the fisherman can be awkward to handle and tricky to stow. The second is that the fisherman doesn't actually work.

If you want a self-stowing anchor that you never have to touch, and operate a boat capable of such an arrangement, the first of these objections may hold a pint or two of water. The second reservation is pure balderdash, always discounting the Christmas-cracker anchors sold as fishermen in certain chandleries. For flukes, these wretched creations have nothing more than the palms banged out flat from the bent bar of the crown. If you're lucky this will have a bit of a point on it. You're unlikely to find an example weighing more than a bumper bag of Big-D peanuts, while the holding power compares unfavourably with a bent pin in a bucket of fine dry sand. No wonder the fisherman has ended up with a bad name.

A real fisherman anchor is substantial and properly forged. Its shank is long, elegant and probably rectangular in cross-section. The crown sweeps round so that the flukes, or palms, end up nearly parallel to the shank, while the stock, which can be dismounted and stowed in line with the shank if necessary, is a meaty bar of pure iron with a short right-angle at one end and, perhaps, heavy iron balls at the extremities. Pulled along the seabed, the stock presents the flukes correctly to the ooze and the lower one has no option but to dig in, and dig in deep.

When I took possession of *Hirta* my 1911 pilot cutter she was blessed with numerous original features. Among these was a one hundredweight (112lb) fisherman anchor date-stamped 1895. It was backed up by 45 fathoms (82 metres) of half-inch (12½ mm) chain. The boat displaced around 35 tons. I owned her for 15 years and sailed her far

and wide. Hundreds of nights passed at anchor and never once did that fisherman drag. In the clear Caribbean I'd swim down and marvel at the sight of the fluke driven into the sand, the shank lying flat along the bottom and the stock controlling the whole business. So effective was this ground tackle that when I built the 20-ton *Westernman* to replace *Hirta*, I specified a 75lb fisherman and 7/16 inch (11 mm) chain. I couldn't find a suitable vintage anchor, so I commissioned a new one from the people who still made them for lifeboats. It wasn't quite as elegant as the original, but in ten years of mixed long-range cruising that one never dragged either.

That's how good fishermen are. They look lovely too, and totally appropriate for our craft. The burning question is, how are we to handle them in the absence of a small army of weightlifters on the foredeck?

The system I inherited on *Hirta* was so effective I never felt the need to alter it. The chain and the vital windlass were sited well aft on the foredeck, feeding a cable locker just forward of the mast. The pilots liked it this way because it kept weight out of the ends of the vessel. The anchor stowed as follows: a hardwood pad was built into the topsides immediately below deck level a few feet forward of the chain plates. One fluke was placed on this pad, the shank ran forward at upper bulwark level and the stock was laid across the oak capping. The top fluke protruded above the capping, but created no issues and looked rather good. Once in place, the anchor was secured by two lashings. The chain cable led sweetly over the bowsprit whisker shrouds, thence to the bow roller on one side of the stem head and inboard to the windlass. The arrangement proved perfectly safe and crossed the Atlantic twice without mishap, including an interesting session with the Greenland Sea.

To hoist this hefty anchor and chain into place on the rail, the shank carried a balance lug in the form of a ring. With the pick up-and-down under the bow, we'd grapple this from the deck with an old-fashioned 'grabbit' on the end of the boathook. This enabled the user to snap a stout hook with a rope on the end into the ring, then remove the boathook pole. The grabbit rope was now attached to the staysail halyard and a few fathoms of chain were surged out to give the anchor enough slack to be hauled aft as well as up. A likely lad was deployed on the halyard purchase, while a lesser mortal bore off as the halyard, the grabbit rope, and finally the anchor rose to capping height. It was guided and lowered into place, then lashed. Nobody had to manhandle anything heavy and the process took only a minute or two. It's standard practice on many big classics to this day. As for us, if we weren't going far and we felt lazy, we'd just hook the trusty fisherman under the bobstay and sail like that. No problem.

So what's all this fuss about fisherman anchors for proper boats? Bring them on, I say and kiss that dragging feeling goodbye!

LEFT: I stowed a 112lb fisherman anchor in this way on my 35-ton cutter for 15 years. It worked without a hitch every time

HOW TO SAIL AN ANCHOR OUT

Much is written about the art of laying an anchor. Quite right too, but what about getting it back aboard? These days, most boats above a certain size feature a windlass, often electric, which makes mincemeat of the job. It's the smaller craft that demand real skill. Foredecks, with room for the luckless crew to lean aft and pull with their thighs as much as their arms, are rare. It's not unusual to end up in the dreaded 'leaning forwards and heaving upwards' position, which more or less guarantees a sprung lumbar muscle. On a bad day, it can mean a full-on back spasm and incapacity.

With a reliable engine, of course, weighing anchor holds no horrors, given a good hand at the helm and sound communication between the ends of the boat. Most of us have long since mastered the art of motoring carefully up to the hook as the foredeck hand gathers in chain. With the cable 'up-and-down', a good burst astern plucks the pick from the seabed, we heave in the tackle and off we jolly well go. Sailing an anchor out requires more sophistication.

I once cruised with an excellent sailing boat displacing something over ten tons with no windlass and no usable engine. Ground

RIGHT: These two paid hands have opted to sail out the anchor using the staysail, not the jib, for a headsail. They're about to hook it under the bobstay for a quick result and so as not to get the foredeck muddy

SEAMANSHIP | 147

tackle was a 35lb CQR with 40 fathoms of 3/8inch chain. For readers of metric persuasion, this translates as a 16kg anchor with 75 metres of 10 mm cable. Any attempt to heave that lot up in a stiff breeze isn't far short of a non-starter, even for a fit 30-year-old. Whoever you are, it's asking for trouble. In those days my wife and I anchored two-up all the time, so we really cracked the process.

The boat was a gaff cutter which gave her a great advantage: she carried her jib on a long bowsprit and, like most of her type, sailed perfectly well without a staysail. With the foredeck clear of a sail banging around she balanced fine, which meant that with the jib sheets led aft we could sail out the hook in relative tranquillity. Here's how it works:

- Hoist main and jib. Coil down. Assuming no tide, the boat is now lying head to wind with everything flogging.
- Overhaul some mainsheet so the boat can bear away, then back the jib.
- With plenty of cable between you and the anchor, the bow falls off smartly and the overhauled main starts to fill as the boat takes up a close-reaching attitude. Don't be tempted to try for close-hauled with the main pinned in. If you do, she will be reluctant to gather way and will simply try to luff up.
- Let draw the jib and sail away on the close reach until the cable snubs. The boat will turn towards the anchor, assisted by the canny helmsperson, until the jib comes aback and whips her onto the other tack. The helm now passes the jib across and sails away again on as close a reach as can be managed, always gaining ground towards the anchor.
- The cable slackens as the boat comes dead downwind of the hook. The foredeck man gathers in the slack until he sees the chain coming up short again. He then holds the cable on a turn.
- The boat tacks again and the process is repeated.
- After coming-about two or three times, the cable is much shorter and as the boat sails across the anchor she pulls it out using nothing more than a round turn and the substantial inertia of her own way.
- She can then heave to, while the hook is brought aboard. The crew wash down, hoist the staysail and crack off for new adventures.

DRYING OUT

Traditional craft have always dried out between tides for scrubbing and minor underwater repairs. At worst, it's cheap. At best, it's free. Perhaps because of the arrival of the short fin keel which may not even be able to bear a boat's weight, people no longer see using the tide as the default for getting at the bottom of the boat, yet for many classics, it works as well as ever it did. Any straight-keeled working craft is made for the job, as are many pre- and early post-war yachts. Assuming a few basic observations and skills, then, why ever not?

First, you must know about the bed you plan to lie on. If it's littered with rocks, supermarket trolleys and rusty bedsteads your experience will not end well, so check it out first. The kindest bottom is a traditional 'hard' of compacted gravel, shingle or clean sand. Proper scrubbing grids work if the keel is long enough to straddle the gaps between the bearers, but a concrete pad is less desirable. Because it has no 'give' at all, it's unsuitable for boats without a straight keel. Also, if it isn't perfectly flat, any long-keeler with inside ballast is going to complain loudly. A fin with a slightly rounded base, or a long keel with 'rocker' won't enjoy the inevitable point loadings either. Both are better off on gravel.

If you think you hate people who leave wakes in harbour, wait until you've been bounced a few times while taking the ground. It gives a new dimension to the word. Seek a quiet berth if you possibly can, and, while you're at it, have a glance at the tide tables. Nothing's worse than being neaped because the next high water doesn't make as much as the one that allowed you to squeak onto the grid. If the tides really are taking off, it may be a fortnight before you float. Try to arrive at the top of the tide or even a little before, especially if there is any doubt about getting on. That way you can retreat in good order if you don't like how things look, and there's plenty of time to get organised if you do.

Many 'hards' offer scrubbing piles to lie against, rather than a more accommodating wall. Walls feel secure, but things can get a bit tight for space on the inside and, if you're planning to antifoul, a wall between the boat and the wind holds up the drying process maddeningly. Piles don't have these problems but they can be challenging for any but a long-keeler.

The crunch for a successful dry-out depends on a satisfactory angle of lean-in. First, sort out your fendering. You're going to need more than a few of the usual nominal plastic sausages. Cram in plenty. If your topsides can take it, a couple of motor tyres are best of all and think about a fender plank on piles. Now move a load of weight such as water jugs or anchor chain onto the deck by the wall. Sailing boats can run a halyard ashore and crank it up as the boat drops with the tide. The ideal inward angle is probably around 3 degrees, but 5 degrees feels safer, as well as doing away with any danger of the dreaded tipping over. Don't forget that the inward angle will increase as the boat's weight begins to bear on the fenders, so be sure not to nip your bulwarks.

Changes in fore and aft trim as the boat settles can introduce unwelcome complications. A traditional yacht with a

long keel running reasonably parallel with the waterline will dry out on a flat bottom without drooping much off her marks. If she has a bit of drag down to the rudder, making her draw more aft than forward, a classic West Country drying berth lying athwart the run of a river accommodates her perfectly. In a berth running with the stream, she'll probably 'pray' to a greater or lesser extent. No problem, so long as you're ready to take up slack or heave in on bow and stern lines. A so-called long-keeler whose profile sweeps up steadily from her rudder post to her forefoot, such as was common in 1930s racing boats of the Dorade type, will have a poor time of things and is best hauled by a yard.

FLAG ETIQUETTE

I well recall a difference of opinion with one of my Yachtmaster Instructor colleagues some years ago. Our boats were rafted up at the end of a long day and my crew were taking in our colours according to the ship's standing orders.

'I can't be bothered with all that stuff,' said my opposite number. 'I seize my ensign to the backstay and leave it there until it rots.'

Sailing the Baltic one day and bringing mine below as usual I was gratified to note a fair number of Swedes, Finns and Danes doing the same. They weren't punctilious about the timing, but a lot more flags were coming down than you'd have seen back in the UK. Sailors who leave their colours flapping idly in the dark are not only bringing dishonour on the ship, they are also raising two fingers in the face of common thrift. 'Colours' isn't an idle institution; it's based on solid history. Samuel Pepys himself, wearing his hat as commissioner of the Navy from 1673 to 1679, decreed that all ships under his control should take in their ensigns at sunset and rehoist at 0800. The reason was simple. Cost. Leaving them up when they couldn't be seen doubled the wear and tear. The bunting bill tumbled, the order has never been rescinded and who are we to argue such an authority?

I'd like the think that among the classic community there's no discussion about this. Most of us go to considerable lengths to maintain traditions and, since lowering colours involves minimal inconvenience, we might as well stick with this one.

Respect for the past has a lot to do with flag etiquette. In my case, it's personal. During the 1980s I became involved with *Cotton Blossom IV*, a Fife yacht of substance run on the east coast of the US by that great English skipper Richard Griffiths. Richard was meticulous about colours, as were his crew. When one of them paid off and signed on with me he brought the discipline with him. The late Robert St John Riddle was an old school yachtsman. In harbour, no matter what social excesses had been heaped upon him the night before, every morning prompt at 0800 he was at the taffrail unfurling our ensign. The same held good in the evening. He never missed. Now that Robert has gone to a well-deserved reward in another bourne

LEFT: A perfect angle for 'lying in' onto the wall makes drying out stress-free. The boys are working fast to beat the tide

from our own, I owe my shipmate the respect of keeping up his work.

There's a quiet satisfaction in lowering the ensign as the sun dips – or at 2100 local time in high latitudes. The courtesy ensign can follow, together with the burgee. As the stick rattles back up the mast the following morning and the ensign staff thumps into its socket, the eight o'clock ritual punctuates the start of the day.

Not everyone has had the privilege of a crew like Robert, but we all know about Samuel Pepys. A decent stitched ensign is not cheap. Why halve its life through sheer indolence?

BURGEES

Forty years ago I was fitting out a substantial old cutter in Cowes. Go back the same time again and you're in the thick of World War II, which puts the timespan into perspective. Nowadays, much of the gear we need is available new, at a price, from classic chandleries. In 1980 nobody was making it, but well-worn original kit could still be found with diligent effort.

Next door to where I was based, at what was once Marvin's Yard, an establishment of character rambled out into the river on rickety piers. Here, where the great yachts had once laid up in serried ranks, it seemed anything might be found and many a useful discovery was trawled from the depths of its sheds. One of these was a Baby Blake toilet that had either been custom built or modified to take to the skies in a Sunderland flying boat. To save weight, many of the bronze parts had been recast in aluminium and the handles were drilled with large holes. Every ounce was pared down except, of course, when it came to the noble ceramic bowl – gentleman's pattern, not one of those wretched round ones. No compromise in quality here and it served me well until the alloy finally succumbed to the inevitable. I binned it on a tropical island far, far away.

A lone survivor of the wonders rescued in those distant days had come my way via an auction one Friday night. After some hot bidding, I took ownership of a burgee stick which I still have. It must have originated from some grand vessel left there for the war and never reclaimed after hostilities. Painted black, the pole is a six-foot (1.8 metre) length of clear hardwood. The bronze swivel carrying the flag is beautifully formed and a snug fit for the stick. It was designed for a serious burgee or a racing pennant with a hoist of 18 inches (46 cm). This makes the metalwork on the big side for my Royal Cruising Club and Old Gaffers Association burgees (alternated, depending on circumstances) which only measure about two foot six (76 cm) on the fly.

The stick, however, proved ideal for the old cutter and has slotted in well on subsequent lesser yachts with taller masts. After all those years and so many thousands of miles, the pole, which started out in as-new condition, is now worn by time and many a masthead sheave, but it still stands proud when asked. The swivel remains in perfect order. It functions in just the same way as those cheap little lightweight affairs you can buy for the dinghy. Made from a single length of bronze rod, the lower end is bent over at 90 degrees into a circle that fits around the stick with a fair gap of slack. The rod then proceeds upwards until it reaches the top. Here, it is bent once again into a much smaller circle. For total happiness, this second circle must be centred over the middle of the top of the stick when the metal upright is parallel with the side. The top of the woodwork is sawn off flat to form a bearing surface.

The swivel is held in place with a simple, but very specific arrangement which I have found works well, even on home-made jobs. A screw-hole is drilled carefully down the centre of the stick to accept a long, round-headed wood screw. One washer (originally bronze, now stainless steel) is seated on top of the stick, below the upper ring of the swivel. A second washer is slipped onto the screw, which is passed down through the swivel ring and the lower washer, then driven home just far enough to leave a gap of perhaps one sixteenth of an inch. This allows full circular motion for the swivel which turns on the washers with no wear that I've ever been able to measure. In the absence of bronze, a swivel suitable for a smaller yacht can be knocked up nowadays out of an extra-strong wire coat hanger. The burgee itself is secured to the upright by whatever means suits best.

A traditional yacht hoists her burgee with a light halyard to a sheave set into the truck of the mainmast. This is ideal because the truck, standing off from the spar as it does, carries the burgee stick out with it. A sheave screwed into the side of a modern aluminium mast never works as well.

The two ends of the halyard will have been tied together so it can't be lost aloft. It is secured to the stick by passing a pair of clove hitches made in the bight, ideally with the knot between the hitches so it can't foul the sheave. Hoisting a burgee on a gaffer is often a challenge. If there's anything that can possibly foul it on the way up, it will find a way. The task is easier head-to-wind on a mooring. In a marina berth with the breeze on the beam it can be a nightmare. Keeping the stick horizontal is often best. Once it's mastheaded, I tension the upper part of the halyard and make it fast. Only then do I set up the lower part which, of course, flips the stick upright to finish the job.

ABOVE: Heaving and swigging are techniques that are readily learned but, outside of big professionally run yachts, they are in danger of becoming lost arts

Sad to relate, after a lifetime of wooden masts with trucks, my current modern classic has a metal spar and a cluttered masthead. So far, I have failed to find a way of flying a burgee among all this nonsense, but I can't live with myself any longer. This year I plan to crack it. My old mate the late Robert St John Riddle would be pleased. When serving with me in the 1980s, he brought in the burgee with the ensign every night, resetting it at 0800 no matter how hung over we might be. Robert was a proper sailor who understood that a yacht is the sum of all the little details her people care about.

Give us a swig, Mate

The healthy thing about halyards on traditional craft is that they come straight down the mast to whoever's hauling up the sail. This means that he or she can use all the available body weight to assist in the task rather than trying to heave horizontally or upwards. I well remember the mainsail hoist on the Yankee schooner that supplied my first professional berth. Until then I'd always imagined one just grabbed the halyard and pulled it. None of that idle stuff was countenanced here. My lively young shipmates positively hurled themselves at the halyards, leaping several feet off the deck to lay hands on the ropes. Gravity did the rest, assisted by their own strength as they bore down after their feet hit the planking. It was a revelation of sheer energy and it can be so effective that I used it in middle age when hoisting an 800 square foot flax gaff mainsail single-handed.

Such theatricals are all very well, but when it comes to getting the last few feet of a halyard home, unless a purchase is rigged on the standing part, there's little choice but to swig it. By far the most effective way to do this is two-handed, with one person on the halyard and the other at the pin or cleat. First, get yourselves organised so you aren't falling over one another. If the gear is really top notch with big pins on a proper rail, the pin man makes a half figure-eight under and up around the pin. His job is going to be to snap up the slack passed down by the swigger, then hold the load so not an inch is lost. As long as the halyard renders sweetly around the pin, the half figure-eight works well and guarantees no loss after the slack is taken up. Many boats don't have this sort of kit, leaving the poor sailor with a bit of iron poked through a timber rail, or a cleat on the side of the mast. If this is your lot, you'll have no joy with the figure-eight. It will jam for sure. Your only hope is to lead the rope under the cleat or pin and hang on like grim death when the big hit of the swigger's effort comes on.

Now for the one doing the swigging. Stand with your feet near the pin, look straight at the halyard, reach forward and grasp it in both hands at face level. On no account reach upwards. The higher you go, the less you will achieve. After making sure your mate isn't going to let the rope slip on the pin and catapult you into the scuppers, throw your whole weight aggressively backwards, taking the bight of the halyard with you as the gaff or the head of the sail nudges upwards. When you're as far back as you can go, lean down on your hands with all your might and move your body back in towards the natural fall of the rope. Your mate grabs the slack you are delivering, holds on while you take a fresh grip on the halyard for another swig, and so on until the sail is up.

Doing the job on your own is a lot less effective, but can still succeed on smaller boats. Your left hand stands in for the guy on the pin, while your right does the swigging. The half-figure-eight has little chance of working in this situation, so it's half a turn under the cleat, heave back with your right hand, grab the slack with your left and hang on until there's no more to be had.

HOLDING A STOPPER

On larger boats where more than one person is needed per halyard on the initial hoist, the fall is led through a turning block into a horizontal pull so that a team can heave away together. You'll see this done on hefty working boats such as the smack *Pioneer* and on big-class classic yachts. Tailing on with all hands aboard the Fife 19-metre *Mariquita* as the crew hoisted the 3,400 square-foot mainsail with a 'stamp and go', roaring out the chorus to 'South Australia' as Captain Thom gave them the lead was an experience not to be forgotten. The question, though, is how to get that massive load from the line-up of muscle to the belaying pin because, with the gaff at full hoist, the halyard is singing like a canary at the turning block. The answer is the magic of the stopper.

A stopper is no more than a length of suitable rope secured at one end to the

deck or to the turning block itself. When the halyard is as far up as it is going to go, the bosun has his moment of glory. Down on his knees, he whips a back turn of the stopper around the halyard above and close to the block. Then he claps on more turns, spiralling upwards around the halyard, winding with the lay of the rope. A few feet up, he takes hold of the stopper and the halyard and squeezes them together with a grip like a vice. The hands back off from the pull and the stopper shoulders the load until the mate has relieved the crowd of the halyard and secured it on its pin. Stopper off, coil down and move on to the next halyard.

Stoppers like this are also used on high-end classics where the initial pull is supplied by a massive powered winch rather than ten hands including the cook, complete with chef's hat, as was the tradition in Edwardian times. The winch has other duties, so the halyard is removed using a stopper, then belayed in the old-fashioned way.

Sculling

The first time I saw a boat being sculled properly was in a race at Bursledon Regatta on the River Hamble back in 1970. We aren't talking single sculls in the Olympics here, with pairs of oars in the hands of trained athletes. What caught my eye was the sight of working men standing in substantial clinker-built boats, blasting them along at remarkable speeds with a single long oar over the stern. Shirts were off and muscles bulged. The boats positively surged from side to side under the combined effort of the sculls and the weight of the contestants. They didn't half shift. At the other end of the scale, also at Bursledon, the foreman of the Elephant yard used to stand quietly in his pram dinghy, pipe in mouth and small curly dog at the bow, sculling in from his old fishing boat one-handed to give his little chum a run ashore. The scene was so tranquil that, however dismal your day had been, things never seemed so bad any more.

Sculling is a dying art, yet it has an important place in traditional boating. For distance work, rowing is less tiring and more effective, but when you arrive alongside a friend's yacht the shortfalls of double oars are instantly obvious. The problem with rowing a tender is that as you round up at the end of the trip, the oar nearest the action must be unshipped. If you have any care for the yacht's topsides, the rowlock has to follow. This annoyance is aggravated when the wet oar comes aboard with attendant nuisance factor. Pilots on the Bristol Channel were always sculled across to ships by their apprentice in a 12-foot punt. Coming alongside the pilot ladder they didn't even have to unship the sculling oar. No matter what the weather, the 'old man' hopped onto the bottom rung, kicked the punt off and away went the lad, sculling back to the parent cutter.

The first essential for successful sculling is a deep notch in the transom. The second is an oar of the right length with a flat, two-sided blade. Finding the length that

LEFT: An old hand at the game can move a boat with effortless ease using only a single oar

works best is really a matter of trial and error, taking into consideration the boat, the height of the transom, your own strength and whether you intend to scull standing or sitting. Sitting is easier for a beginner, so we'll stick with that, but it's still impossible to be dogmatic about oar length because much will depend on the distance from the transom to the thwart on which you perch.

Sit facing sideways, legs astride the thwart. Settle the oar into the sculling notch and raise your end of it to shoulder height. Grasp it lightly with your aft hand in an overhand grip and move the submerged blade well out to one side. Now incline the blade by rolling the wrist so that, when you move it across the transom the inclination presses it down into the water. As it shunts across, it will be shoved deep into the notch and won't try to escape. This consumes half the force, the rest creates a reaction that converts into forward motion. The clever bit comes at the end of the stroke. The wrist is rolled the other way as far as it will turn so that the oar blade presents its reverse face to the water in the same attitude as before. Push it back across, roll the wrist again and so on. A rhythm soon develops that is as ancient as man's efforts to propel boats on water. Once you've cracked it, it is pure harmony.

Let's not allow this traditional skill to sink into history. That magic flick of the hand rapidly becomes a motor function you can execute in your sleep. You'll have become part of an exclusive band; you might even join the rarefied world of those who stand up to the job with both hands, ripping into the task and creating a serious bow wave.

Hoisting the dinghy aboard

If you sail a traditional craft with space enough to stow a hard dinghy, spare a thought for the poor souls condemned to go ashore with a wet bottom, courtesy of the flubber that serves instead of a nice clinker punt. The only upside to these creations of Satan is that they can be stowed in places a real dinghy cannot. A proper ship's boat is superior in every other way, although in the absence of stern davits it does ask questions about launching and recovery.

LIFTING BOLTS

The first consideration is the eyes to which the lifting strop is secured. In an ideal world, these will be ring bolts, all inside the boat. The bow unit should be high on the stem, although practicality often means that the external towing ring for the painter is used instead. This can work, so long as it isn't sited too low, but the stern lifting points must make up for the inevitable resulting shortfall in balance. Aft, the bolts are best set through the transom, one either side. A sophisticated outfit will have a dedicated lifting strop that shackles to these and ends in a ring amidships, joining with a further pre-measured line coming from the stem. When hooked to a halyard, the ring stands several feet above the gunwale.

RIGHT: When davits are employed, different lifting points may be used instead of the ideal single-halyard lift eyes described above

Personally, I've never got around to making these strops. A lash-up of bow and stern painters served me adequately for decades. If you favour this low-cost method, you'll need a loop to attach the halyard. I've seen people tying figures of eight for this. Have nothing to do with such unseamanlike practice. Use a bowline in the bight. It's simple to make and easy to break after the serious weight of the lift.

LIFTING POWER

While it's sometimes possible to manhandle a dinghy over the rail and onto the deck, lifting it under control is more civilised. For reasons of weight distribution and convenience of working around it when stowed, tenders usually end up more or less amidships, abaft the mast. For a gaffer, this makes the throat halyard the crane of choice. While inferior to a dedicated davit, it is sited conveniently and, as the most powerful tackle on the ship, can supply plenty of power.

Bermudan yachts usually opt for the main halyard led to its own winch. This can be hard labour compared with the gaffer's heave-ho because winding a winch depends on muscle, whereas pulling down on a halyard relies more on the scientific application of body weight. The gaff option is therefore recommended for those who prefer not to make regular visits to the gym.

A classier answer, favoured by motor yachts and larger sailing craft, is the dedicated davit. This will be swung out over the boat by its guys and secured in place. The hoist will probably have a simple purchase with the fall led to the windlass or some other handy power source. Once the punt is above deck level, it is swung inboard with the guys and lowered onto its chocks. The davit makes the job easy, doing away with the issues created by using a halyard on a task for which it was never designed.

BEARING OFF

If you don't have a davit – and most boats don't – lifting the dinghy with a halyard means that, left to its own devices, it will graunch against the topsides as it travels up or down. The force of the lift isn't vertical, so it resolves itself into two. Direct upward pull is what we want, but a second force, smaller but significant, is dragging inwards. On all but the biggest yachts with seriously heavy tenders, the easiest way of neutralising this is to fender the action, then station the strongest person available immediately inboard of the halyard after it has been attached to the lifting strop. As lesser mortals heave away on the halyard and the boat ascends from the water, Charles Atlas leans out on the rope or parts of the tackle, bearing the punt off the planking as it rises by walking his hands down the halyard, the strop and finally the boat itself. Once it is clear of the capping, he can step carefully back and allow the inward component to swing it across the deck. With the load still on the halyard, he and his shipmates can then manoeuvre it above the chocks and lower away.

WHICH WAY UP?
Upside down

In a perfect world, dinghies are stowed on deck bottom up for the self-evident reason that a ton or two of breaking sea cannot come thundering into them, with all the attendant horrors. The best way to turn a heavy punt whose lifting rings are inboard, is to lower it gingerly, heaving down on one side so that it finally takes its own weight while standing on one gunwale. The halyard can then be eased progressively so that the crew take over the load on the uphill side and lower the boat into the chocks. Practice is needed to land the punt initially in the right spot for this to succeed without grunting and cursing, but when executed tidily it is a joy to watch.

Right way up

Upside down stowage may be best, but it's a deal easier just to lower the boat away and settle her with her keel in the chocks. She then offers a desperate bosun a handy place to dispose of unstowable items like fenders, heavy warps and the skipper's bicycle. Covered neatly, she'll look fine, the bosun's shame will not be obvious and none but the most persistent seas will get at her. The bungs must, of course, be left open. If she has no bungs I would hesitate to stow her right way up, for reasons that should be as clear as bilge water pumping out of a leaky boat.

Purchases – an extra part for nothing

A purchase with two double blocks – one with a becket for securing the standing end – can be rove to advantage, at 5:1, or disadvantage, at 4:1. If the purchase is the mainsheet – with one block at the bottom and no quarter blocks – it will probably be rove to disadvantage with the becket block at the bottom, because that way the fall comes off a sheave at deck level where it can readily be secured. Shackle the becket block to the boom and you have 5:1 all right, but making up the fall at some fixed point on deck is untidy, especially if the lower block slides on a horse. The fall inevitably comes 'flying' out of a sheave on the boom end block, and tension alters as the boom moves across.

Norwegians, Dutchmen and Thames barge skippers have had the answer to this for over a century. In the Netherlands, lower mainsheet blocks have a horn on the cheek for making up the fall. Norwegians and barges are less decorative, but equally effective. Their lower mainsheet blocks – all running on horses – have an extra-long pin for belaying the fall.

I once decided to increase the power of a mainsheet running on a horse by the simple expedient of swapping the blocks over, then banging an extra-long bolt through the lower one in place of the pin. It worked for years.

BULL ROPES

All boats moored or anchored in tidal waters suffer from 'sailing' ahead over the ground tackle when the breeze sets in against the stream. Spoon-bowed yachts lose paint off their topsides on the chain and I've seen all sorts of lash-ups with fenders that never quite seem to work. A plumb-stemmed boat suffers even more. She hardly has to move before she's into the buoy or graunching ahead with her anchor chain, chewing the planking above and below the waterline. The sorry owners of modern yachts can do little about this misery, but many of us traditional boaters are privileged to carry bowsprits, and the bowsprit holds the answer.

Hang a single block from the end of the spar. Run a line out to it from the foredeck and attach the lower end to the mooring buoy or the bight of the anchor chain. Heave the line fairly short, depending on bowsprit length, so that when the boat runs over her anchor, instead of the cable clattering down the topsides from the bow roller, it is guided silently out of trouble from the bowsprit end. In heavy conditions, the topmast forestay may find itself 'doing a good job', in which case set up the runners to stop the rig nodding like the heads of a tennis crowd.

ABOVE: A bull rope has ensured a quiet night's sleep for many a foremast hand, as well as protecting the mooring strop and the bobstay

SECURING A ROPE

Whether it's a cleat, a belaying pin, a bollard or a ring in a dock wall, there will always be someone shouting the odds about how a line must be secured. They may be right on the day or, very likely, they'll be wrong, because the secret of successfully making lines off is not to preach specific methods, but to ask yourself what you're trying to achieve.

My own criteria are simple: a rope that's made fast must be secure and remain so until the time comes to release it. Then, it should be easy to remove the turns, even when loaded, until the line can be eased or surged under perfect control.

A popular, one-size-fits-all solution for a cleat is promoted by the OXO brigade – 'One round turn, one figure of eight, then jam on a second round turn that slips in under the others at the bottom of the cleat to hold it all together'. This is often sound enough, but it won't work if the rope is too big for the cleat supplied, or if you don't have enough of it. In such a case, you will often be constrained to clap on a single locking hitch by turning the second half of a figure-of-eight over on itself and snugging it tight. Which brings us to the Great Locking Hitch Controversy and the 'no locking hitches' police.

I'm old enough to have sailed on a small ship rigged entirely with natural fibre cordage. We soon learned to use locking hitches only with the greatest circumspection because, once the stuff shrank in the rain, it had a habit of seizing in place. It was then unmovable without a spike. Not what you want when you're letting go the topsail halyard in a hurry to save a topmast that's bending like Robin Hood's longbow poised to dish the Sheriff of Nottingham. That was 50 years ago and it was out of date even then. Modern cordage does not shrink in the rain or even when soaked with salt water. It may go stiff over the years, but it won't jam unless the user commits some major atrocity. There is therefore no reason to damn the ever-useful locking hitch out of hand. Lifting one off a pin or cleat may take a second longer than otherwise, so if this matters, don't use one unless you have to.

Often, it poses no problem at all, and the locking hitch provides an extra layer of security. Any halyard belayed where a sea can wash over it is going to be a lot safer with a locking hitch, whether it's on a ship's fife rail or a cleat aboard a tiny yacht. Mark you, the hitch must be the right way round, following the preceding figure of eight sweetly. Steer well clear of those nasty in-line efforts guaranteed to slip when it really counts.

The final word on locking hitches goes to my old shipmate, the late Captain George Moffett of the US schooner *Brilliant*. He had just won the Transatlantic Tall Ships' Race and I was aboard as pilot for the English Channel. I noticed that every rope on board, be it halyard, downhaul or sheet, was secured with a locking hitch. When I asked why, he replied that with trainees it made sense to promote a standardised system, adding that he'd never had one let go or jam. You can't say fairer than that, can you?

Meanwhile, what about the pundits who insist on securing a shoreline to a perfectly good pontoon cleat with a round turn and two half hitches. God only knows where they went to school, and don't get me started on the no-sailors who jam two ropes onto the same cleat when they don't absolutely have to.

I may like to see certain systems employed on vessels where more than one person will be attending to a belay in pitch darkness. It's always good to know what to expect, but in the privacy of your own boat, I don't care how many turns or hitches you use or don't use. So long as it's secure and can be eased under load, it'll do for me.

RIGHT: With no kicking strap or vang, and only rudimentary spinnaker pole foreguys, classic yachts were not always easy to control on a heavy-airs run in their heyday

Marking the anchor cable

Anchor aboard any modern yacht and you'll find that somebody has misguidedly marked the chain in metres, very likely every five. Back when depths were sounded in fathoms, cable was marked in similar proportions but because a fathom is almost two metres it was a lot less fussy and easier to read. I still use fathoms for my chain, starting at ten. You'll never lay less cable than that, so mark it, add a generous dab of gash paint every five thereafter and you're done. Your sounder will read in metres, but you've only to divide by two, add a bit for luck and you're back in honest measurement where the unit was the span of a man's arms.

A bullseye aloft

Ever had problems on your gaffer with throat or peak halyards getting mixed up with the gaff jaws? You won't be alone if you have, and the trouble doesn't end there. All sorts of lines coming down to the deck on any traditional boat can chafe. A tip I picked up years ago in Norway solved this for me. Find an old-fashioned bullseye, seize it to a shroud or a spreader and lead the offending line through it, clear of trouble. You might imagine that the seizing would never stand the strain of a tensioned peak halyard fall, but all it's doing is shifting the pull from dead straight to a few degrees 'off-centre'. It makes no difference to the efficiency of the halyard and it never lets go.

Offset propellers

Any pure sailing boat built without an auxiliary engine in mind almost certainly has too fine a run to accept a centrally sited engine and stern gear. The result, if a motor is subsequently fitted, will be an offset propeller.

Some offset props result in handling that is the stuff of nightmares, but if thoughtfully installed by people who know their business, side propellers conforming to certain rules can be a pleasure. One boat I used to sail was an archetypal case in point. Her habits with little way on were predictable, but I only learned about the dynamics after a few years of what are best described as varied results. The boat drew 8 feet and had a right-handed propeller under her port quarter, sited a few feet forward of a noble, full-length rudder. As we all know, a right-hand prop running in reverse shows a natural tendency to throw the stern to port. This is because it chucks out wash to starboard. With what amounted to a wall of boat sitting on the prop's starboard side at slow speeds, however, the prop's efforts to cartwheel to port were in vain. Its wash hit the near-vertical planking and bounced out to port instead. There was nowhere else for it to go. As it came gushing out, the stern was tossed in the opposite direction and the boat spun accordingly. 'Starboard side to the dock' was therefore a joy for her.

By 'backing and filling' ahead and astern with the rudder hard over to port all the time, she would turn to port in just a few feet more than her overall length. It was marvellous.

I only discovered the interesting bit years later when I found myself careering into the dreaded port-side-to berth without the option and the wind behind me. In desperation, I threw her into astern at four knots and, behold, she snuggled her stern in to port like a Bavaria 37. It seemed unbelievable until I worked out what happened. At that speed, the prop wash never hit the boat at all, it just spiralled off the prop and did what it had wanted to all along. Ever after, when I had to come port side to, I arrived at a velocity which terrified the onlookers, but which I knew was my only hope. Thank goodness the gearbox never let me down.

GLOSSARY

ALL STANDING | A term of description relating to any action taken without proper preparation. Thus, to gybe all standing, is to allow the boom to crash across without any attempt to control it on the mainsheet. An all-standing gybe in the grandest sense would involve backstays left made up. In such a case the results could prove catastrophic.

ARCHER, COLIN 1832–1921 | Born in Norway of Scottish parents, he was perhaps the greatest designer of working vessels of all time. Boats are still built to his concepts. His life-saving craft have never been beaten for seaworthiness, while his pilot boats were a glory of speed, beauty and strength. Sadly, his name is often taken in vain, and many, though not all, so-called 'Colin Archer types' do not perform so well.

BECKET | The fitting on a block to which a rope may be attached.

BIGHT | The middle part of a rope, between the belay and the load. Sometimes the term is used to define a loop of rope, or even a loop of the coastline as in 'German Bight'.

BITTS | These are massive baulks of timber, stepped deep down in the vessel (ideally on the keel), with their upper ends protruding through the foredeck. They are used for the bowsprit heel and sometimes form the basis of a traditional windlass, as well as being excellent for towing or tying up.

BOBSTAY | Standing rigging that supports a bowsprit from below.

BOLSTERS | Hardwood chocks running fore and aft bearing down on the upper surface of the cheeks which keep the main shrouds in place at the hounds.

BOOT TOP | A line painted between the antifouling on the bottom of the boat and the topside, paint above the water.

BRAIL | These are ropes which serve to gather up a standing gaff sail or a spritsail, spilling wind from it and stowing it against the mast and the gaff. They run inboard from the leech of the sail to turning blocks on the spars. They are handled from the deck.

BULLDOG GRIPS | These are really a highly-developed form of U-bolt for holding two wires firmly together. They can be used to make a permanent job, and boats have circumnavigated (notably Bernard Moitessier in *Joshua*) with nothing but bulldogs to hold the rigging together.

BULLSEYE | A fair-lead made of a sphere of hardwood, drilled and chamfered for the rope to pass through. The outside of the sphere is scored all round to take a strop which may be of rope or iron. Bullseyes are usually of lignum vitae.

BURTON | A purchase set up on the fall of another purchase to multiply its load.

CAMBER | The flow, or curvature, of a sail when seen in a cross section cut at right-angles to the mast. The maximum camber should be about 40% of the way from luff to leech on most sails.

CAVIL | A horizontal bar, usually of wood, spanning and extending beyond two through-deck stanchions inside the bulwarks, forming a strong point for belaying.

CHANNELS | Blocks, usually of wood, often supported by ironwork, outboard on the planking or at deck level. They are used to spread the shroud base in narrow vessels.

CHEEK BLOCK | A single sheave built onto the side of a spar.

CLEW | The lower leeward corner of a sail to which the sheet is attached.

CLUB | A short spar laced to the aft end of the foot of a sail which is otherwise loosefooted. It serves two main functions. One is to extend the sail beyond its natural sheeting position, thus gaining area. The other, which is really a spin-off, is that the operator has a choice of attaching the sheet anywhere along the club, which assists in the search for a good sheet-lead. Clubs are used on staysails for sloops, and sometimes on a loose-footed schooner foresail, but they are found more commonly on the foot of a topsail, where they are more properly known as 'jackyards'.

COMB | An arrangement, usually in hardwood, built onto the sides of a boom at the extreme end to facilitate the reefing gear.

COVERING BOARD | This is a heavy plank at the edge of the deck on a traditionally built wooden boat, so-called because it covers the upper surface of the top plank of the hull, also known as the sheer strake.

CRANSE IRON | A hoop of iron driven onto a shoulder at the outboard end of the bowsprit. For a fully rigged spar the cranse would have four lugs (small rings) welded to it for the attachment of standing rigging.

CRINGLE | A reinforced attachment point used on a sail in places where heavy loads are expected, such as tack, clew, throat, peak and the sites of attachment of reefing pennants at tack and clew. Traditionally, rope grommets worked around thimbles, cringles today may simply be stamped through the cloth and strengthened with tabling. Not to be confused with eyes, or eyelets which are reinforced smaller holes for lacing.

DEADEYE | A substantial circular block of wood, always found in pairs, through which shroud lanyards pass in order to set up the standing rigging on a traditional vessel.

FALL | That part of a purchase which is pulled by the operator. A double-ended halyard has two falls. One is the hauling end, by which the sail is taken aloft. The other is the standing end, on which is rigged a further purchase, supplying the tension for the whole assembly.

FIDDED TOPMAST | An extension upwards of a mast, so called because it is stopped from descending by a fid, or iron spike upon which it sits, or which is passed through its lower sections.

FIDDLE | A raised rail at the edge of a table or a work surface to prevent objects sliding off at sea.

FLAKE | A means of folding a sail as it comes down, or laying out a rope so that it can run cleanly when required.

FOREFOOT | The part of a vessel's underwater profile between the stem and the straight part of the keel. If the keel never does straighten out, as is the case with certain yachts, it can be considered as the part of the underwater form forward of the mast.

FULL-RIGGED SHIP | Any three-masted vessel which is square-rigged on all three masts is technically a 'ship'. All other permutations place a vessel into a different category, such as barque, barquentine, three-masted topsail schooner, etc.

GAFF JAWS | Curved wooden members mounted on either side of the forward end of the gaff to locate it on the mast. A more sophisticated metal version is known as a gaff saddle.

GAMMON IRON | The hoop at the stem through which the bowsprit is passed. The term goes back to the days when bowsprits were lashed down to the stem by a system of well-organised ropework called gammoning.

GOOSENECK | The metal fitting which supplies universal movement between boom and mast. Some booms do not have a gooseneck, preferring instead a set of jaws similar to those of the gaff. These sit on a wooden shelf around the mast when at rest.

GROUND TACKLE | Anchors, chains, rodes and anything appertaining to the process of anchoring. In this context tackle is pronounced as spelled with a short 'a'.

HANDY BILLY | A travelling tackle which can be set up wherever extra purchase is needed. The stationary block often has a useful shackle or hook, while the moving block carries a lanyard which is rolling hitched to the rope to be pulled.

HEAD DOWNHAUL | A light line secured to the head of a jib or staysail, brought down to the deck via a turning block near the tack of the sail. It enables the sail to be pulled down positively after letting go the halyard, then secured in the lowered position.

HELM 'DOWN' AND 'UP' | The term applies to the way a tiller, if there is one, would be pushed for any particular manoeuvre. For example, the helm is put down (to leeward) when the boat tacks. It is put up (to windward) for a gybe. The terminology passes through unchanged to wheel steering. Regardless of which way the wheel is turned, the helm is still put 'down' if the boat is to turn to windward, and vice-versa.

HORSE | A sort of bridge set above the deck or a boom, through-bolted at both ends, along which an attachment may slide. The horse for a mainsail clew would be of iron, and the main part of its length (about 18in on a 21ft boom) runs parallel to the upper surface of the boom. Horses are also used for sheets, notably mainsheets and staysail sheets. Sheet horses run athwartships and are usually of iron, though exceptionally they may be of heavy timber, as in the Thames sailing barge.

HOUNDS | The part of the mast to which the main shrouds are attached. In a gaffer it is well up the shaft, because it must be above the gaff jaws.

JACKYARD | *See* Club.

JACKYARDER | Name in general use for a jackyard topsail, this being a topsail whose luff and foot are both extended, the luff by the topsail yard and the foot by the jackyard.

JIB-BOOM | An extension to the bowsprit of a basically similar form to a topmast. It is held in place by spectacle irons (see note), and carries a full set of shrouds and stays. It does not normally bear a vessel's main forestay.

JIB-HEADED | As the name suggests, a jib-headed sail is pointed at the top. It is entirely innocent of yards or headsticks.

LACING | This is a length of light line used to attach a sail to a spar along its length. It may be found on booms, gaffs or sometimes masts on gaff rig vessels.

LANYARD | A light cord to hold something, such as a knife, often connected to a belt. Lanyards are also used for securing awnings and many other items.

LAZY JACKS | Lines led from aloft to pass around the main boom in order to control the sail as it is lowered, preparatory to securing it with ties.

LEECH | The trailing or leeward edge of a sail.

LIFTING | The luff of a sail is said to lift when it first begins to be backwinded.

LIZARD | A hardwood bullseye attached to a length of line, used for adjusting the angle of a sheet.

LOOSE-FOOTED | A sail whose foot is not laced to a spar, but is attached only at tack and clew. A loose-footed sail may be set without any boom at all, with the sheet attached directly to the clew, or it may be set on a boom. In this case, the clew attaches to the boom which is controlled by the sheet.

LUFF | The leading or windward edge of a sail.

OVERHAUL | The friction inherent in any tackle makes pulling it out by heaving on one of its blocks hard work. If the rope is worked through beforehand so that the tackle lies slack, the job becomes very much easier. This process is known as overhauling. Sometimes, all that is necessary to overhaul is to let off the fall of a purchase before a sail is dropped, but if you want slack on the mainsheet before topping up the boom, you'll have to pull it through as described.

PARCELLING | A galvanised wire splice is always in danger from rust. Parcelling is part of the process of protection and is typically carried out by wrapping canvas soaked in tar around the vulnerable area. The wire is first 'wormed' with a length of spunyarn to fill up the gap in the lay. The parcel is finished with a serving laid on as follows: 'Worm and parcel with the lay, turn and serve the other way.'

PARREL BALLS | Small, hardwood spheres drilled to accept a rope.

PEAK | The top aft corner of the gaff sail. The peak halyards raise the aft part of the gaff. They also control the angle the spar is making with the mast.

PENNANT | Sometimes 'Pendant' or 'Penant'. A line which serves to haul down the clew reef cringle.

PURCHASE | The tackle rigged to the standing end of a two-ended halyard.

RACKING SEIZING | A seizing designed so that only one of the two wires seized together takes the load.

RATLINES | Lines rigged fore and aft between the shrouds of a sailing vessel, to form a ladder.

SCANDALISE | A method of quickly reducing the area of a mainsail. Usually a gaff sail. The universal system is to ease the peak halyards. A better arrangement is to trice the tack up the mast using a line rigged below the gaff jaws.

SEIZING | A seizing is a sophisticated form of lashing which holds two ropes or wires together, side by side.

SHEAVE | The wheel part of a pulley block. Sometimes a sheave is let into a spar, as in the case of the main clew outhaul or the bowsprit traveller outhaul.

SHEERPOLE | The sheerpoles run fore-and-aft, joining together the shrouds immediately above the upper deadeyes or the rigging screws. They can be lashed or bolted on. Their official function is to stop the shrouds from sheering, or twisting, but they also serve as useful places to carry belaying pins from which to hang halyards at sea. They form a conveniently sturdy bottom step for the ratlines.

SHROUD | Standing rigging, usually wire, rigged athwartships to support a mast.

SPLICE | To make a loop in a rope's end without using a knot. A splice can also be used for attaching two ropes together or various other functions.

SPREADER | A small spar rigged horizontally athwartships from a mast to spread the load of the athwartships rigging or shrouds.

STAYSAIL | A triangular sail rigged from one of the forestays of a mast.

STOPPER | In this instance, the stopper is a length of rope rolling-hitched to the bight of the halyard, with possibly a couple more half-hitches around to back up the main hitch. To be really sure, the stopper can be wormed round with the lay before leaving the halyard after a final half-hitch. The end of the stopper is now hauled tight and belayed. It will hold the bight of the halyard until it has been belayed; then the stopper is let off and removed. The principle of the stopper has numerous applications.

SURGE | To allow a loaded rope to render around a cleat or bollard under control.

SWIG | To throw one's weight outboard from a halyard or a sheet, thus achieving a stronger pull than simply using the shoulders.

TACK DOWNHAUL | A strop attached to the tack of a jib allowing it to travel some distance up the stay. A tack-downhaul is generally passed through a turning block on the bowsprit end and attached to a tackle on deck so that the luff may be tensioned.

TACKLE | Pronounced 'taykle', this is an arrangement of blocks (pulleys) and ropes, rove up to give a mechanical advantage.

THROAT | The upper forward corner of a gaff sail is

always known as the throat. Thus, the throat halyard is the forward of the two gaff halyards.

TOPPING LIFT | A rope which supports the weight of the boom when it is not being carried by the sail.

TRAVELLER | In this context a traveller is a forged, leathered ring which runs up and down around the bowsprit.

TRICING LINE | A light line generally used for pulling a length of rigging, not currently loaded, away from the action. Typical examples are the bobstay at anchor and the lee running backstay. A tricing line is used through a turning block at the gaff jaws for heaving up the tack of a hooped mainsail to improve visibility or reduce sail quickly.

TRUCK | The wooden cap which protects the end grain of a timber mast.

VANG | In traditional craft, a vang is a rope which controls the movement of the outboard end of a gaff or sprit. Sprit rigs have two of these, one each side, and sailors pronounce them as wangs. Gaff vangs are pronounced as spelled, and generally only one is rigged per spar.

WALE | A heavy topside plank on a working vessel running fore and aft under the chainplates, sometimes referred to as a wale strake.

WHIP | A single block hanging from a rope. By reeving a line through it and dead-ending one end, the resulting power which is applied to the load is 2:1. Whips are effective because with only one sheave involved, friction is cut to a minimum.

INDEX

Admiralty Manual of Seamanship 34
anchors/anchoring
    fisherman 143, 145
    marking anchor cable 166
    sailing an anchor out 146, 148
antifreeze 134–5
Archer, Colin 54, 61, 107
autopilot 107

Baby Blake toilets 152
ballast, movable 104–5
barometers 88–9
beeswax 138
Bermudan yachts 10, 12, 17, 19, 27, 28, 35, 38, 40, 45, 58, 60, 61, 66, 79, 83, 160
blocks
    maintaining brightwork 122, 124–6
    maintaining performance 126, 128–9
    purchase systems 161
    servicing 126, 128–9
bobstays 54–5
bolts, seized 115
boom angle 50
boom gallows 105–6
boomed staysail 31–2
boot tops 131
Boracol 115–16
bosun's chairs/harnesses 34, 48, 134
bosun's role, traditional 6, 9
bowsprits 53–6
    bobstays 54–5
    bull ropes 162
    heel ropes 54
    netting 20
    simple handles 54
    staying offset bowsprits 55–6
    topmast forestays 55

tricing lines 54–5
brightwork, treating 122, 124–6
Bristol Channel pilot cutters 39, 50, 105, 120, 157
bull ropes 162
bullseyes 21, 66, 67, 167
burgees 152–4
Burnett, Ed 56
burton 42–3
Butler, Harrison 56, 131

cabin stoves/heating 99
caulking deck seams 119–20
chafing, sailcloth stitching and 47
chain plates 102–3
chairs/harness, bosun's 34, 48, 134
Chloe May 20
clews, dragging 29–30
club yard 21, 23
coils, hanging 42
compasses 84, 86, 89
Cooke, Francis B 142–3
cookers 99
Cotton Blossom IV 151
cove lines 132
cutter foretriangles 28

davits 160
dead reckoning 89
deadeyes 37, 52–3
deck seam maintenance 119–20
Deks Olje 125, 137
dinghies
    hoisting aboard 158, 160–1
    stowing 161
    towing 142–3
downhauling 24
drying out and underwater repairs 149, 151
Dyarchy forestays 56–8

engines, idle 134–5
ensigns 151–2
eye splices 36

fiddles 92–4
fisherman anchors 143, 145
flag etiquette 151–2
flaking 79, 82–3
forestays, Dyarchy 56–8
foretriangles and windward sailing, setting up 26–8
Fox, Uffa 12
friction tape 37

gaff rigs 12, 17–18, 21, 45
galley stoves 99
gangion 36, 48
gaskets 81–2
Giles, Jack Laurent 56, 58
Griffiths, Maurice 21, 104
Griffiths, Richard 151
guardrails and stanchions 76, 78–9
Gunning, Max 107

halyards
    bullseyes and clearance from gaff jaws 167
    drying out process 149, 151
    Dyarchy forestay 56–8
    flaking 79, 82–3
    hoisting burgees 152–3
    lifting dinghies 158, 160–1
    locking hitches 163
    and rigging 53, 56–7
    and sails 15, 18, 28, 69, 79, 157
    scandalising 18
    stoppers 155, 157
    stopping rattles 83
    swigging 154–5
harbour-stowing staysails 72–3
Harrison Butler 56, 131
Hasler, Col. 'Blondie' 106–7
Heard, Martin 131
heel ropes 54
hemp and manila replicas 36, 62
Herreshoff, Nathanael 20
Hesper 20
Hirta 93, 120, 126, 143, 145

Hiscock, Eric 140
hoisting the sail 15
hounds 35, 38, 45, 132, 134

Italian hemp lanyards 40

jackyard topsails 21, 23
Jeffery's Marine Glue 118, 120–1
Jester 106
jib luffs 28, 50, 57
jib-stay 57
Jolie Brise 20, 45, 74, 99, 106

keeping watch 109–10

lacing 17
ladders *see* ratlines
lamps, oil 94, 99
lanolin 115
lanyards 21, 40, 52–3
laying up ashore, benefits of 132
lazy jacks 62
leader 24
leaking chain plates 102
leaking decks 116–18
lignum vitae deadeyes 52
linseed oil 114, 122, 137
lizards 21, 66–7
locking hitches 163
logbooks 86–8
luff, tensioning topsail 56–7
luff yard 23, 24

Mackrill, Martyn 11, 21, 61, 84
mainsheet arrangements
　full-width mainsheet horse 61
　single attachment point 60
　'snubber and quarter-block' solution 60–1
maintenance 112–38
　beeswax 138
　boats in winter 132, 134–6
　boot tops 131
　cove lines 132
　deck seams 119–20
　getting rid of green growth 115–16

idle machinery 134–5
lanolin 115, 129, 137
leaking decks 116–18
nails 138
pouring pitch 120–1
rust 138
seized bolts 115
slush and wire rigging 114
stopping up 121–2
tallow 114–15
treating brightwork 122, 124–6
useful bits and pieces 138
wale strakes 131–2
wooden block performance 126, 128–9
manila rope 36
Mariquita 155
marline, tarred 36, 48
Martin, E G 47
mast hoops 17, 68–9
mast rakes 50
mastheads, sagging 110
masts over winter 132, 134
modern yachts 18, 69, 70, 76, 79, 83, 89, 103, 109, 162, 166
　see also Bermudan yachts
Moffett, Captain George 163
moorings, wind against 69
muriatic acid 138

nails 138
navigation 84–9
　barometers 86
　classic logbooks 86–8
　dead reckoning 89
　improvisation 89
　ship's compass 84, 86
Nightfall 21, 23

offset propellers 167
oil lamps 94, 99

patent sheaves 126, 128, 129
pennants, reef 70–2
Pepys, Samuel 151–2
Pinckney, Roger 56, 58
pine tar oil 124
Piskie 24

planking 10, 102–3, 162
ply 109
polypropylene rope 36, 48, 62
propellers, offset 167
pulpits and pushpits 78

rainwater 38
ratlines 34–7
　method 36–7
　the objective 35–6
　ropes 36
　shrouds 36–7
　tarred marline or synthetic substitutes 36
reef combs 70–2
reefing mainsails 69–72
Riddle, Robert St John 151, 154
rigging 34–62
　baggywrinkle 47–8
　Burton poles 42–3
　deadeyes 52–3
　Dyarchy forestays 56–8
　housing bowsprits 53–6
　logbook notes 88
　mainsheet arrangements 58, 60–1
　mast rake 50
　ratlines 34–7
　rope types 36, 47–8, 61
　sheer poles 37, 40, 42
　slush and wire rigging 114
　spreaders 45, 47
　stainless steel 34, 37
　throat crane 38–9
　topping lifts 61–2
ring bolts 158
ropes
　bull 162
　securing 163–4
　types 36, 47–8, 61
　Dyneema® fibre 43, 55, 58, 71, 78–9
rot 36, 38, 72, 81, 102, 134
Royal Yacht Association (RYA) 34
rust 138

Saari 23, 107, 109

INDEX

safety regulations 76
sagging mastheads 110
sails 12–32
   boomed staysail 31–2
   burgees 152–4
   downhauling topsails 24
   dragging clews 29–30
   flaking 79, 81–3
   harbour-stowing staysails 72–3
   hoisting 15
   jackyard 19, 21, 23
   luff yard 23, 24
   reef pennants 70–2
   reefing mainsails 69–72
   sail ties 81–2
   setting a single luff spinnaker 14
   setting up the foretriangle when sailing windward 26–8
   single headsails 27–8
   stoppers 155, 157
   stowing 72–3, 79, 81
   topsail overlap 24
   topsails 21, 23–4
   tricing or scandalising gaff mainsails 17–18, 68
   watersails 24, 26
   Yankee jibs 19–21, 66
sawdust and weeping seams 110
scandalising or tricing gaff mainsails 17–18, 68
scrubbing piles 149
sculling 157–8
seacocks, frozen 135

seamanship 140–67
   anchors 143, 145, 146, 148
   bull ropes 162
   bullseyes and halyard clearance 167
   burgees 152–4
   defined 140
   drying out for repairs 149, 151
   fisherman anchors 143, 145
   flag etiquette 151–2
   hoisting aboard and stowing 140, 145, 158, 160–1
   hoisting sail 154–5, 157
   marking anchor cable 166
   offset propellers 167
   purchase systems and blocks 161
   sculling 157–8
   securing ropes 163–4
   stoppers 155, 157
   swigging 154–5
   towing dinghies 142–3
   see also working the ship
seizings, racking 36–7
sheaves 126, 128–9
sheer poles 37, 40, 42
shrouds 40, 42, 45
single headsails 27–8
single-luff spinnakers, setting 14
single topping lifts 18, 61–2
Skeates, Nick 31
Sleightholme, J D 21
Slocum, Captain Joshua 114
slush/animal fat, use of 114–15
Smyth, Admiral W H 40, 42
spreaders 45, 47
stanchions and guardrails 76, 78–9
staysail, boomed 31–2
staysails, stowing 72–3
Stockholm tar 112, 114, 134
stoppers 155, 157
stowing sails 79, 80
'swifters' 50
swigging 154–5
synthetic ropes *see* rope types

tallow 114–15
tarred marline or synthetic substitutes 36, 48
The Tempest (W Shakespeare) 9
throat crane 38–9
tiller lines 74, 76
topmasts forestays 55
topping lifts 61–2
topsails 21, 23–4
towing dinghies 142–3
tricing line, bowsprit 54–5
tricing or scandalising gaff mainsails 17–18, 68
turning blocks 56–7, 58, 66, 68, 70
turpentine 114, 124, 137
twin topping lifts 18, 61, 105

vangs, rig 29
varnish 106, 122, 124–5, 126
Varnol 124–5
Velsia 54

wale strakes 131–2
watchkeeping 109–10
watersails 24, 26
wax 138
weather helm and movable ballast 103–4
Westernman 20, 24, 26, 28, 39, 68, 74, 102, 104, 105, 145
Westward 20
whip, rigging 24
windage 47
windvane self-steering 106–7, 108
wintering boats 132, 134–5
working the ship 64–83
   flaking halyards 79, 82–3
   harbour-stowing staysails 72–3
   jib topsails 20, 66, 78
   lizards 66–7
   mast hoops 68–9
   reefing the mainsail 69–72
   sail ties 81–2
   stanchions and guardrails 76, 78–9
   stopping halyards rattling 83
   tiller lines 74, 76
   tricing mainsails 68
   wind against tide mooring and scandalising 69
Worth, Claud 38, 39
Wylo II 31

Yankee jibs 19–21, 66

Zinnia 58